The Psycho 100

The Psycho 100

Baseball's Most Outrageous Moments

Steve Lyons and Burton Rocks

TRIUMPH
BOOKS

Triumph Books and colophon are registered trademarks of Random House, Inc.

Library of Congress Cataloging-in-Publication Data

Lyons, Steve.
 The psycho 100 : baseball's most outrageous moments / Steve Lyons and Burton Rocks.
   p. cm.
 ISBN 978-1-60078-167-4
 1. Baseball—Miscellanea. I. Rocks, Burton. II. Title. III. Title: Psycho one hundred.
 GV873.L97 2009
 796.357—dc22

                          2008042187

This book is available in quantity at special discounts for your group or organization. For further information, contact:

   Triumph Books
   542 South Dearborn Street
   Suite 750
   Chicago, Illinois 60605
   (312) 939-3330
   Fax (312) 663-3557

Printed in U.S.A.
ISBN: 978-1-60078-167-4
Design by Jill Petrowsky
Page production by Patricia Frey
Photos courtesy of AP Images unless otherwise indicated.

To baseball fans everywhere who find the funnier, crazier, and zanier side of baseball entertaining

You gotta be a man to play baseball for a living, but you gotta have a lot of little boy in you, too.

—Roy Campanella

Contents

Acknowledgments

I'd like to thank the hundreds of people who contributed to this book by recalling and sharing their favorite crazy moments with me. Fans, coworkers, players, coaches, managers, vendors, and front office people—anybody and everybody who had seen a game of baseball and was willing to reminisce and smile. Thanks also to Tom Bast, Adam Motin, Don Gulbrandsen, and the entire staff at Triumph Books and Random House for making this book a reality. To my coauthor and agent, Burton Rocks, who was the original catalyst behind the idea and a tireless ball of energy. A special thanks to my girlfriend, Debi, for her patience and to my youngest daughter, Ally, for all the missed dinners and games of "speed" while I hunted and pecked. As always, I'm grateful to my entire family, including my mom and dad, my three brothers, my three daughters, and my grandson for their support in all that I try.

—Steve Lyons

CHAPTER ONE

Getting Caught with Your Pants Down

Psycho Becomes a Household Name

How many times do you think I've told this story? Do you think I'm tired of telling it? Well, to answer that question, I'd pose another: does Mick Jagger get tired of singing "Satisfaction"?

He better not.

I know it's a big stretch to compare myself to the Stones, but sometimes careers are launched on a single moment or a single song. So you're just a jerk if you don't appreciate the interest that gets generated from that moment, and now get annoyed or tired of talking about it.

So yeah, people have asked me about pulling my pants down on the field every day of my life since it happened—and that was in 1990! But I don't mind talking about it. It was one of the craziest plays ever—maybe *the* craziest.

It truly was one of those "Oh my god, I was at that game!" moments. So let's set the record straight for all the Red Sox fans that have told me they were at the game in Boston and for the White Sox fans that say they saw me do it in Chicago. Maybe 15,000 people actually saw it happen, but 100,000 people have told me they were there.

I was playing for the White Sox in Detroit. It was a usual day—I was already 0-for-1 and looking for a way to avoid going 0-for-4 against Tigers starter Dan Petry. So I dragged a bunt with me to the first-base side of the field. I could tell that Lou Whitaker, the second baseman, got a good jump on the ball, but I also got big first baseman Cecil Fielder to commit to the ball as well. Now I knew it was going to be a race to the first-base bag with the pitcher, Petry, because he was going to have to cover.

Sure enough, the instincts kicked in and I dove for the first-base bag. I probably did that about 50 times in my whole career; sometimes I was hoping to make it a tougher call for the umpire, sometimes I was hoping he'd have sympathy and call me safe on sheer effort alone. Well, this time the ball, Petry, and I all got to first at just about the same time, and as my body and Petry's right foot each touched the bag, we both looked up to see the umpire, Jim Evans, yell "Safe!"

Petry went nuts—as well he should have, because I think he did beat me to the base, and he and Evans got into it face to face. I hopped up knowing no matter what Petry said, Evans wasn't going to change the call. Sweet! Safe at first and 1-for-2.

The problem was that when I slid into first, a lot of little pebbles and infield dirt went right down the front of my pants, and when I stood up they all rushed down my pant legs toward my socks (or Sox, if you prefer). With Petry and Evans still creating a commotion right there in front of me, I literally forgot I was standing before 15,000 fans and did what anybody would do—I started shaking the dirt out of my pants. I undid the belt, unsnapped the snaps of my pants, and even unzipped the zipper. With the first tug, my pants fell to around my knees. With another tug, my pants crumpled down around my ankles. Then it hit me. Bent over and nearly naked from the waist down, the only thing between me and an X rating was my sliding shorts! In a flash, I had those pants back up around my waist where they belonged. Cecil Fielder was laughing, the argument between Petry and Evans came to a screeching halt, and now I was standing there feeling even more naked than I was just seconds ago! I don't get embarrassed easily, but there I was, just as red as could be. The only thing I could do was just start laughing along with everybody else. I tucked in my shirt, buttoned up my pants, and cinched up my belt,

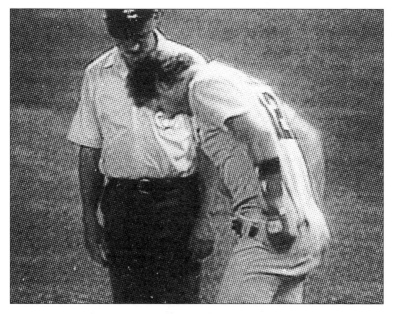

A Psycho is born one embarrassing day in Detroit. Photo courtesy of Steve Lyons.

not knowing that play would end up being the defining moment of my career.

The next guy bounced into a force play and I was out at second. When I got back to the dugout, women were waving dollar bills at me and yelling "Take it off!" My teammate Jack McDowell suggested I get an off-season job as an exotic dancer.

It was an innocent brain cramp, but it got so much attention. My manager, Jeff Torborg, was slightly peeved at me because he didn't really see what happened and thought I had done it on purpose. Johnny Carson made a joke about me in his monologue the next night, and David Letterman approached me about being on his show. I did 32 radio interviews throughout the next day and seven live newscasts from Tiger Stadium before the next night's game. *Playgirl* called (I declined). A few weeks later, *Sports Illustrated* did an article called "Moon Man" all about the incident. All of that…for what? Because I got dirt in my pants? Five days earlier, one of our pitchers, Melido Perez, threw a no-hitter in Yankee Stadium. It seemed like nobody noticed, but I show off my underwear…

People always ask me, "What were you thinking?" or "Are you gonna keep your pants on today?" The amazing part is that every one of those people thinks they're the first person to ever ask. It's okay—if it amuses them, then that's fine.

The fact is I had this bad habit of sliding headfirst into first base on close plays. I would get all excited about the possibility of actually getting a hit, and the closer I got to the base, the more I wanted to get there any way I could! Save the lectures about how it's faster to run through the base—I've heard 'em all and it's probably true. But if it is, why does an outfielder dive for a line drive that's a little out of his reach? He's trying to get there faster.

After all these years what everybody else remembers about that bizarre play is that I pulled my pants down on the field—nobody had ever done that before.

What I remember is that I was safe.

Tommy Lasorda Takes a Bad Hop

What hasn't Tommy Lasorda done? Think about it: Tommy played in the big leagues, won championships during a Hall of Fame managing career, guided the US Olympic team to a gold medal, and is the greatest living ambassador of baseball today.

Of course, his favorite team is the Dodgers. And he'll let you know it loud and clear. He was a celebrity guest singer of "Take Me

Tommy Lasorda gets a face full of turf at the 2001 All-Star Game. Photo courtesy of Getty Images.

Out to the Ballgame" at Chicago's famed Wrigley Field in 2008, and instead of saying "root, root, root for the Cubbies," Lasorda belted out "root, root, root for the Dodgers!" The fans laughed. Then they booed. They knew that he just couldn't put on a false face. He was Tommy Lasorda, bleeder of Dodger Blue. Even his answering machine years ago at Dodger Stadium ended with, "And you have to root for the Dodgers." He's even gone so far as to tell people that they may not go to heaven if they're not a Dodgers fan!

But this story isn't about Tommy the legend.

This is about one of the craziest scenes ever witnessed at an All-Star Game—in Seattle in 2001, to be exact. You remember the one—A-Rod moved over to third so Cal Ripken Jr. could start at shortstop for one last All-Star Game, and then Cal played the hero by crushing a home run.

I covered that game and was hanging around in the NL dugout when Tommy, who was an honorary coach, decided he wanted to coach third base like he did back in the old days. I think everybody thought it was a great idea—that's how Tommy got his start, out there waving the boys home and creating some excitement.

Don Zimmer was over in the AL dugout, and he was laughing his butt off at the sight of Lasorda back on the field.

Tommy suddenly screamed at Zim, "I don't see you dragging your old bones out here to do it. I'm gonna help get this team some runs!"

(Of course, Tommy used more colorful language—I had to clean it up for the purposes of these pages.)

Soon enough, however, the Expos' Vladimir Guerrero stepped up to the plate. I don't think you can name too many pitchers in the game who don't shudder just a little bit when they have to face Vladimir with runners on base.

Vicious free swinger that he is, Vlad took his hacks one powerful swing at a time. But Guerrero took one particularly wild swing at a slider down and away and lost his grip on the bat. This is not uncommon, and usually it's no big deal. But this time the business end of Vlad's Louisville Slugger headed directly right at 73-year-old Tommy Lasorda!

Tommy didn't know which way to go or how to get out of the way of the oncoming missile. The bat seemed to be on a collision course with his head.

Back when I played in the late '80s and early '90s, an "ugly finder" is what we used to call a ball or bat that hit anyone.

Luckily for Tommy, Vlad's bat ricocheted right past him. The bat ended up hitting right in front of Tommy as he tumbled backward.

Lasorda lost his hat, his balance, and just a little of his dignity.

In my book (and this is my book), the entire play should have been ruled an error!

In 2009, Tommy will begin his 60th year as part of the Dodgers family.

The National Leaguers couldn't get a replacement third-base coach out there fast enough.

I'm happy it turned out the way it did because it could have resulted in a serious injury for Lasorda.

But I don't think Zimmer was thinking of that, because if you thought he was laughing hard when Tommy went out there to coach, you should have seen him after his friend went rolling around on the turf.

Hang in there, Tommy—you're still the best.

Canseco Finally Uses His Head

While May 26, 1993, might not be a significant day in the history of the game, it certainly was a significant day in Jose Canseco's infamous career. Not too many guys get to be part of a home run by having the ball bounce off their noggins and over the wall!

I'm actually hoping that when it's all said and done, Canseco is more widely known for this blunder than his post-baseball career. Sure you know the story, and based on how crazy it was, the ball bouncing off his head and over the wall for a homer will rank right up there with any of the other crazy moments in this book. He was tracking a fly ball deep into right field and somehow lost sight of where it was until it bounced off his head and hopped over the wall for a home run…blah, blah, blah.

But let me digress just a little: I haven't read either of the books Canseco has written—I wouldn't give him the satisfaction or my money. And I believe that a lot of what he says in the books is probably true. But to me, that's not the point. The worst thing anybody can ever say about you as an athlete is that you're a bad teammate. You've heard it a million times, but that's because it's true—being on a team is exactly like being a member of a family. And when you take your dirty laundry out of the clubhouse and air it in public, without any regard for how it may affect somebody else's life, I take issue with that. It makes me sick to think that some people actually praise Canseco for blowing the top off the steroid problem and bringing it to light. Bull. That book was written for attention, to hurt people, and to somehow suggest that baseball was blacklisting Canseco because he couldn't find a job. And yet I don't believe he ever takes the time to thank the game that granted him a life of privilege and luxury. I would have more respect for him if he had come out in the middle of one of his big-money contracts and admitted that he was using steroids then. That would have taken guts. Instead he reaped the benefits, hid his lies, and banked the money—then pointed fingers at everybody else when things got tough.

Of course, Jose's moved on to great things now, like getting his butt kicked in the boxing ring by former NFL player–turned–broadcaster Vai Sikahema and being detained at the Mexican border trying to smuggle in illegal drugs.

Sorry for my digression; I suppose I could go on and on with more details and even more disdain, but I'll end it here. I think that for all the fame and all the money and all the broken promises that epitomized Jose Canseco, living with the guilt and looking into the mirror right now must be pretty painful.

Fair or Foul?

Those who know anything about me know that I'm a big fan of the umpires. No, really, I am! I think they are ridiculously good at what they do. They have to call a bang-bang play at first or whether a pitch is a strike...right now! No replays (unless it's a home-run call). No seven camera angles that everyone at home can see. No slow motion.

You want that job? Thought so.

Having said that, sometimes...they're wrong.

And I suppose things get magnified when you're wrong in Yankee Stadium.

Being a color analyst, I never actually get to make the home-run call. I know, it sucks. But if I did on May 18, 2008, when Carlos Delgado's home run was taken away, it might have gone something like this: "There it goes! Kiss the kids, he's on his way...it's...gone! No, wait...it's foul! No...it's...uhh..."

Come on! What the heck is it? Is it fair or foul? We don't have all night!

No huge surprise that during the heat of the 2008 Subway Series between the Yankees and the Mets, controversy would rear its head.

Delgado smashed a home run that just nicked the foul pole and then landed in foul territory. Or did it?

We thought it did on television, but it was overruled after a conference between the umpires. They got together, as they do if there is a controversial play, to see if one of the umpires had a better view than the one who actually has authority over the call. They do this to make sure they have the best chance of getting the call right. It was ruled a foul ball. I think they were wrong.

As of August 2008 we now have instant replay. I don't like it because of what it represents: that somehow the players and the umpires that govern the game can't get it right or get along. I dislike football for the very same reason—some crybaby fan thinks his team got cheated because an official blew a call late in the game. One call or one play never beats any team. And as my father taught me when I was eight years old (take note of this people), an umpire will *never* beat you. I think what it comes down to is looking yourself in the mirror and owning up to who you are and what you've done. If you're somebody who complains about the officiating of a particular game, then you're a loser yourself. It is as simple as that. Your team had plenty of chances during the course of the entire game to put themselves in a position where one play or one call wouldn't change the outcome of their game. If you lose a game, do what the players today call it: "Wear it."

Jerry Manuel took over the Mets after Willie Randolph was fired in June 2008.

Of course, the replays in baseball are only for ruling on whether a ball is fair or foul. I guess I can live with that—unfortunately for Delgado, he hit his home run...er, foul ball...before replay came into the picture.

Delgado had to step back into the batter's box and try again. The strangest part about the whole play was that the umpire closest to the play called it a home run, but the home-plate umpire overruled him.

Mets bench coach Jerry Manuel protested and got himself thrown out of the game.

A fan sitting in the seat next to the yellow foul pole in left field had snared the ball after it ricocheted off the pole. On national television, he pointed out the mark the ball made on the foul pole. There it was, plain and simple and in plain view. There was the mark on the ball from the pole, and there was the mark on the foul pole from the ball. Oops!

ESPN made further note of the fan's proof, and Jon Miller and Joe Morgan discussed the play forever, focusing on one reporter interviewing the fan at his seat. Confused about why the outfield umpire was being overruled by the crew chief, everybody was a little miffed.

Still, the call stood. The ball was ruled a foul ball and Delgado had to come back to the plate to hit again. He came through with a hit, but it's a far cry from a home run! Take it from a guy who only hit 19 homers in his whole career—you don't want to give any of them back. Lucky for the umpires that the game wasn't decided by that blown call.

And just to be fair, umpire Bob Davidson admitted after the game that they made the wrong call.

Two for the Price of One

The last thing Mets catcher Paul Lo Duca expected in Game 1 of the 2006 NLDS was that he would be tagging two guys out at the plate on the same play. But that's exactly what happened during a crazy October at Shea.

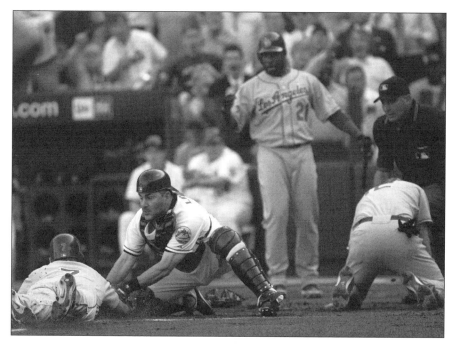

First come, first served: Paul Lo Duca tags out Jeff Kent and J.D. Drew in New York. Photo courtesy of WireImage.

Everyone gets a bit nervous in the playoffs. Performing under those tense circumstances separates the men from the boys—the winners move on and the losers get months of second-guessing and early tee times.

For the Dodgers, there were a couple of guys involved who you would think should have enough experience to avoid a play like this. Jeff Kent is a guy I see on a daily basis. He runs hard, he plays hard, he works hard, and he deserves to be a first-ballot Hall of Famer. He's not a happy guy and rarely smiles, but you still want him on your team. J.D. Drew is a guy who has a reputation as a "tin man"—lots of talent, but no heart. I'm not 100 percent sure I agree with that assessment, but it seems like teams pay him a lot of money and he doesn't give them a lot of fire and gets hurt all the time. Check his numbers at the end of the year and judge for yourself; I think he's gone a long way toward changing that perception, but first impressions last.

It was the top of the second inning at Shea, Kent on second, Drew on first, and nobody out. Russell Martin, the Dodgers' All-Star catcher, hit a shot down the right-field line. Shawn Green, the Mets' right fielder and a former Dodger, ran over and played the carom off the blue wall in right field.

Rich Donnelly was the third-base coach for the Dodgers. When Green came up with the ball, he thought about holding Kent at third but sent him because J.D. was charging up Kent's ass like a bull.

Seeing the "Go!" sign from his coach, Kent rounded third and headed home, but Drew was right on his heels. Donnelly threw his hands up in the air to try to stop Drew, but J.D. was so close to Kent that he ran right through the sign.

The relay throw to the plate was flawless, and Lo Duca was just waiting there at home—with nothing better to do than tag out Kent and then, within a few seconds, tag out Drew, who had roared home and slid right behind Kent.

Grady Little, the Dodgers' manager, was fuming. Donnelly couldn't believe it. The Mets celebrated. What a way for a road team to run themselves out of an inning in the opening game of a series.

Little said that it was a blunder. Billy Wagner, in his *New York Post* column, couldn't believe it happened. Lo Duca, to this day, remains shocked that he is one of the few men to tag out two runners at home plate on the same play.

Russell Martin prefers not to remember the play. Why would he? It was the beginning of the end for the Dodgers and their postseason hopes for that year—and besides, Martin smoked that ball and was hoping for some RBIs. Instead, all he got was a nightmare and a place in my book.

Ahhhh, the playoffs…gotta love 'em.

Kruk Gives Up

John Kruk was a Philadelphia Phillie in every sense of the word. He was tough both on and off the field, even battling back from cancer before parlaying his All-Star career into a second life as a pretty good broadcaster. But in addition to his perseverance, his determination, and his skills as an athlete and survivor, he provided one humorous moment that left everybody in stitches and delights fans every time it shows up on the highlight reels.

Kruk did his best Steve McQueen impersonation as the guy with the helmet on backward ready for battle, but to no avail. More like *Major League* than *The Great Escape*, Kruk showed us all that Randy Johnson is just flat-out scary.

Kruk was never known as a shrinking violet when he played. A good guy off the field, he was a fierce competitor on it and an outstanding hitter.

But Kruk was playing in the 1993 All-Star Game and was at the plate facing Randy Johnson. Kruk had never faced the Big Unit; he'd only heard the terrifying stories from other lefties who had. Johnson immediately blew two mid-90s fastballs by Kruk that John barely even saw. Then Randy uncorked one that went over Kruk's head and all the way to the backstop! John's heart was already pounding after the first two, and now he's thinking his life might be in danger. He

John Kruk tips his hat to Randy Johnson during the 1993 All-Star Game.
Photo courtesy of Getty Images.

stepped out of the batter's box, laughing along with the crowd about the predicament he found himself in. He knew he had no chance at hitting Johnson, so when he got back in the box, he planted himself about four feet away from home plate and out of harm's way. Even Johnson cracked a smile, which he never does when he's pitching. So having him right where he wanted him, Johnson then broke off a slider that was two feet outside and totally unhittable—and Kruk swung at it anyway.

Randy Johnson has more than 4,700 strikeouts in his 21-year career.

That was enough for John. Even if that hadn't been strike three, I don't think he wanted any more chances to hit. He playfully tossed his helmet to the ground and took a bow. What else could he do? He had been totally dominated by one of the most talented pitchers of all time.

Larry Walker Jumps the Gun

I used to enjoy signing autographs for kids and tossing balls into the crowd. I mean, what else did I have to do? I probably wasn't playing that day anyway. I still do it today. I'll grab a baseball from the bag at the stadium and find a kid who has that "I want a real baseball" look in his eyes and give it to him. I usually sign it too, whether he wants me to or not!

But Larry Walker took the idea of giving a kid a ball to an entirely new level back in 1994.

In fact, Walker's move turned an ordinary Sunday night game into a memorable moment for anyone who saw it.

Dodger Stadium is about as laid-back as a stadium can get. Fans arrive in the second inning and leave in the seventh. (Not really, but that's what everybody thinks.) They show up, watch the game, have a beer, and watch the beautiful people go by. But Larry Walker got people to sit up and take notice.

A fly ball was hit to right field and slightly toward the line. Walker, after making a nice running catch, thought he had just caught the third out of the inning, so he gave a kid in the stands the baseball as he trotted toward the dugout.

When he saw the runner on second tagging up and advancing toward third, he realized there were only *two* outs! Larry ran back over to the stands, yanked the ball back from the kid, and threw the ball back into the infield. Unfortunately for him, the umpires awarded the runner two bases since the ball had left the field of play.

Poor Larry! The crowd kept reminding him how many outs there were for the rest of that series. For a while he became a walking blooper reel, and a new generation of fans knew him as the nice outfielder who gave a kid a ball *during* the game.

It was one of those feel-good moments in baseball that are truly authentic. I'm big into authenticity because each year the players and fans, for economic and security reasons, get a bit more removed from each other. This moment reminds us of the fact that while the game of baseball is a billion-dollar business, it's also our national pastime, and the only way to grow the game is to make it as kid-friendly as possible. Players like Larry Walker make sure of that, whether they know how many outs there are or not.

Joe Niekro Files His Nails... and the Ball

Joe Niekro is pretty much known for one thing: throwing a wicked knuckleball. Not a good heater or a knee-buckling hook. Joe was a master of the knuckleball.

So how do you get kicked out of a game for using an emery board to file your nails?

Joe was pitching for the Minnesota Twins on August 3, 1987 against the California Angels—yes, they were called the California Angels once upon a time—when he got caught with his hand in the cookie jar.

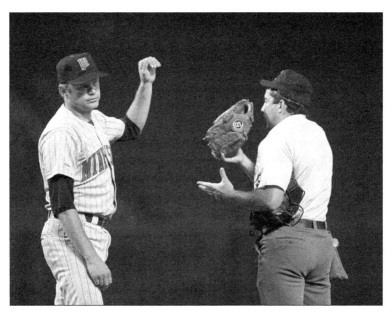

Joe Niekro's knuckleball got some extra knuckling courtesy of a nail file in 1987.

Niekro was on the mound working his magic, but the California hitters began to question whether the magic was real or if Joe was being helped by a foreign substance. Back in the day, baseball managers used to do anything they could to rattle opposing pitchers within the rules of the game. Managers tried to distract the opposing pitcher or the rest of the team by making stupid requests and protests. Doing stuff like that today is considered bush-league and it rarely happens anymore, thank god.

So Niekro was asked by the home-plate umpire, Tim Tschida, to show him his glove. Tschida also asked Niekro to empty his pockets, and that's when the fun started. As soon as Joe reached into his back pockets, a small object flew out of his hand and landed in the grass. Joe kind of held his arms out as if to say, "Gee, where'd that thing come from?"

It turned out that "thing" was an emery board.

Niekro was immediately ejected from the game. Joe humorously maintained that he used the emery board not to scuff baseballs but to manicure his nails so that he could throw his signature knuckleball. But Bobby Brown, the commissioner of the American League, suspended Niekro for 10 games when he found out that five other balls confiscated from that game all had markings from Niekro's emery board. I guess Joe wasn't using that nail file on his nails after all!

Although that incident is the only thing a lot of people remember about Niekro, he should be remembered for much more. He won more than 20 games twice and was an All-Star in 1979. He beat the Dodgers in a one-game playoff game in 1980 that put the Astros into the postseason for the first time in their history. And he was a member of the world championship Twins team in 1987, the same year as the emery board fiasco. He didn't win quite as many games as his Hall of Fame brother Phil, but 221 wins in 22 seasons wasn't too shabby.

I always knew that if there was a knuckleball pitcher on the other team, I was going to have to face him—nobody else wanted to. Charlie Hough was the guy I faced the most: just six hits in 22 at-bats. I was 2-for-10 against Phil Niekro and, believe it or not, I went 3-for-4 against Joe. He must have thrown me some fastballs!

The whole saga did get Niekro on *Late Night with David Letterman*, where Niekro entertained Letterman with a power sander and Vaseline. Sadly, Joe passed away in October of 2006.

Tommy John's Three-Error Play

A lot of guys have made several errors in a single game and I can guarantee you that after their second error of the night, all they were thinking was, *Please, don't hit the ball to me!* But what if you don't have a chance to worry about that next error? What if you make three errors on *one play*?

When he played shortstop, Ozzie Guillen used to tell the pitchers to just pitch and not worry about trying to catch the ball. He thought pitchers were "non-athletes" and that it was his job to field the ball and all the pitcher could do was mess things up. Not a bad theory—especially since Ozzie caught everything in sight. Unfortunately for the Yankees back in July 1988, pitching legend Tommy John just couldn't help himself.

The Yankees were playing the Milwaukee Brewers and John, the aging former All-Star pitcher, took the mound. Joel Skinner was

John's teammate at the time and still laughs to this day about his battery mate's miscue.

"It was the most amazing thing I had ever seen," Joel says. "Tommy gets a routine ground ball hit back at him and scoops it up but then bobbles it to the point where the play is over. He should have just held it and eaten the error, but instead he threw wildly to first. We're all thinking, *What the heck is he doing?* The ball sails past first base and into right field and the runners advance. Fortunately for us, the right fielder snagged that ball and fired home. But Tommy cut off the throw! He threw home himself and threw wildly past our catcher! Three errors in one play! I told my teammates, and I talk about it to this day, that I've never seen anything like it. We love Tommy, but that play takes the cake."

Tommy John won 288 games in his big-league career.

Tommy John wasn't a terrible fielder during his career, and he made only one more error during the 1988 season. Too bad the three he made on a single play are the ones everyone remembers.

Bernie Williams Takes a Curtain Call

If you think I'm the only guy who's ever been on a baseball field half-dressed, think again.

It was the last day of the 1998 season. Joe DiMaggio was honored at Yankee Stadium and was about to address the crowd…but the microphone didn't work! Joe was fuming mad and left in a huff. Wow. What a way to treat one of your legends.

That should have been an omen that the day would be filled with the unexpected.

Bernie Williams was fighting for a batting title and thought he had lost it. After his last at-bat, he was taken out of the game and headed back to the clubhouse.

Bernie retired in 2006 after 16 years with the Yankees.

Little did he know that the guy he was battling for the title, Boston's Mo Vaughn, didn't have a good day at the plate either, and Bernie wound up winning the crown with a .339 average.

The Yankee fans thought that it might be the last time they saw their center fielder in a Yankee uniform. Negotiations between George Steinbrenner and Bernie's agent, Scott Boras, were not going well and it looked like Bernie's days in pinstripes were over.

So the fans chanted "Bernie! Bernie!" and they wouldn't stop until their hero came back out to acknowledge them.

Players in the dugout quickly scrambled to get Williams. They found him half-dressed in the locker room. Having no time to get back into his uniform, Bernie ran back up the steps and stepped onto the field in his uniform pants, an undershirt, and his shower slippers!

Talk about a sweet curtain call!

And maybe those fans had more power than they thought. After the season, Williams signed a seven-year, $87.5-million contract to stay in the Bronx.

A-Rod Says "Boo!"

So did Alex Rodriguez yell "Boo!" or "I got it!" or "Ha!"? We'll never really know the truth, but who really cares? Why is it that when A-Rod does something like that, everybody calls it bush-league or unsportsmanlike?

I guess A-Rod has had more than his fair share of questionable moments. Remember the time he and Paul Lo Duca of the Mets jawed a bit during interleague play in 2006? He also swatted at Red Sox pitcher Bronson Arroyo's glove in a playoff game to try to get him to drop the ball—it worked, but the umpires ruled interference and called A-Rod out anyway. There were those rumors out of both Seattle and Texas that he was often aloof and disliked by his

Alex Rodriguez and John McDonald discuss the meaning of the word "boo" in Toronto. Photo courtesy of WireImage.

teammates. Even his former best friend and teammate, Derek Jeter, barely talks to him. I don't get it. In my mind, he's one of the greatest players of our generation, and maybe of all time. He's certainly the odds-on favorite to become the new Home-Run King in a few years. He posts MVP numbers every year. What's not to like?

But there he was in 2007, between shortstop and third base in Toronto, making sure that he could add new enemies to the growing list. A-Rod yelled something at Blue Jays third baseman Howie Clark, who was camped out under a pop-up, and whatever Rodriguez said made Clark think shortstop John MacDonald was calling him off. He wasn't. The ball dropped and Clark was charged with an error. Then the good stuff started. Clark was pissed at himself for falling for the gag, and mad at Rodriguez for trying it in the first place. Both Clark and MacDonald were yappin' at A-Rod for a play they thought belonged in Little League.

After the game, Toronto manager John Gibbons said he couldn't understand why a classy organization like the Yankees would employ "bush-league tactics." Clark and the Blue Jays were crying about the play for days to come, while A-Rod just continued to do what he does—perform at a high level under a cloud of envy, jealousy, and bad feelings.

You can't keep him off the front page of the tabloids and he's almost always a headliner in the sports section as well. His divorce, the exotic dancer in Toronto, his "friendship" with Madonna—there's always gonna be something to talk about with A-Rod, but that's par for the course when you're the best baseball player on the planet.

Me? I thought it was a pretty creative way to get a guy to drop a routine pop-up and keep an inning going.

George Brett Gets Picked Off of First after His 3,000th Hit

One of the players that I most respected was George Brett. I loved watching him play, I loved playing against him, and I loved having the opportunity to talk to him. When I was a rookie with Boston in 1985, I witnessed one of the most impressive displays of hitting courtesy of Brett and my teammate, Wade Boggs.

Throughout the season, it seemed like when Brett hit a double, Boggs would hit a double. If Brett laced a rocket down the left-field line, Boggs would match him. It was so much fun to see two guys who were great hitters and good friends go at each other as if they were the only ones playing the game. We couldn't wait for one of them to come to the plate to see what they would do next. Hit after hit kept coming for both of those guys, year after year, and they both ended up with more than 3,000 hits, which is a magical number for any hitter. Speaking of magic, Boggs' 3,000th hit was a home run!

But this story is about Brett's landmark hit, and how what should have been a wonderful memory became one for the blooper reels.

It had to be extra special for Brett to get his 3,000th hit against the then-California Angels, just a few miles from where he grew up in El Segundo. His brother Ken, who George always said was a better player than he was, was an Angels announcer and was calling the game.

When he came to the plate at 2,999, Brett faced Tim Fortugno, and promptly banged out a base hit, his fourth of the day. The crowd went crazy even though the game was in California. Brett was one of the best-loved players in the game and this was a milestone moment. Everybody there was so happy to have witnessed the feat and they wanted to let him know what they thought of him. Brett stood at first soaking up the love, tipping his hat and smiling, probably allowing himself to finally think that he maybe he did belong in the Hall of Fame (George was famous for joking that he didn't think he was good enough to get there).

But then an embarrassing thing happened—Fortugno picked Brett off first base! Yep, one of the greatest hitters of my generation got his 3,000th hit and then took one too many steps off the bag at first and…bang!

Very embarrassing, but pretty funny, too. Even Brett had to crack a smile.

I know what you're thinking—where did he think he was going? Brett wasn't necessarily known as a base stealer—he only stole 201 in his whole career and he was caught 97 times.

CHAPTER TWO

What a Play!

Derek Jeter Runs Full Speed into the Stands

I've seen guys charge balls hit to them. I've seen guys run backward and climb the outfield wall. I've seen guys slide just short of the walls in foul territory. But I'd never seen a shortstop run clear past a third baseman and charge full speed into the stands and almost knock himself out cold—that is, until Derek Jeter did it on July 1, 2004.

The pop-up was hit between Jeter and Alex Rodriguez. Jeter called him off, but the ball kept drifting and drifting and drifting. All of a sudden, Jeter found himself face-first in the third-base stands, being helped up by a woman a few rows off the field.

Yankee fans know their baseball, so even if an opposing player does something fantastic, they'll applaud. But when Jeter, their favorite player, raced into the stands and had to leave the game bruised, they honored him as only Yankee fans would.

The very next home game thousands of fans showed up to the ballpark with bandages on their chins and fake bruised eyes. It was the funniest and most clever way I've seen a baseball player's grit honored and appreciated by the fans.

Jeter's play got national media attention, and for good reason. It was another example of Jeter's instincts taking over. The natural fear that would have made most athletes stop and quit on the ball made Jeter want that ball even more. I've heard many a talk-show host downplay the notion of intangibles. I feel that Derek Jeter is living proof of how important intangibles are. Jeter is a player who plays the game on 100 percent instinct. Fortunately for him, his instincts happen to be flawless.

Derek Jeter cements his status as a Yankee legend with this catch against Boston in 2004.

That play was not just another great catch. It was a symbol of how Jeter plays the game and how he helped the Yankees build a new dynasty. What would have happened if he'd have let that ball go foul? It wouldn't have hurt his career. It would have been a foul ball and the hitter would have been given new life. Maybe the guy makes an easy out on a ground ball, but maybe he crushes the next pitch for a home run that hurts the Yankees. Jeter is a team player. For him, it's about saving runs whenever he's in the field. Anyone who thinks that Jeter doesn't have range ought to think again. I call running 95 feet from shortstop to the left-field stands pretty good range!

Thrown Out by a Glove

During the 1986 season, when the Mets were making their magic at Shea, a San Francisco Giants rookie named Terry Mulholland got some national attention for a play that could only be described as pure instinct. A pitcher, Mulholland snagged a comebacker and was ready to make the easy toss to first. The only problem was that he couldn't get the ball out of his glove! It got stuck in the web and Terry had to think fast. So he ran halfway to first base and then tossed the *glove* over for the out.

But that doesn't really compare to what Orlando "El Duque" Hernandez did in 1999. While he claims it was no big deal, it was a big deal because it was not a short, underhanded toss like Mulholland's was. It was a Brett Favre–like overhand pass, and it happened in the middle of a intensely heated Subway Series game between the Mets and Yankees.

El Duque is one of the many players who have played for both the Yankees and the Mets during their careers.

Maybe it was no big deal for a guy like El Duque, who had escaped Fidel Castro on a small boat and was stranded at sea for days. This guy is truly a survivor, and he's got things in perspective. There can be no greater test of survival than the real-life drama of having to save one's family and flee their country. Orlando Hernandez has truly lived the American dream by escaping a dictatorship and playing baseball as a professional in the free world.

El Duque might have thought his play was no big deal, but as far as the Mets and Yankees were concerned, he had launched himself into the middle of an all-out borough war between the Bronx and Queens.

The interleague Subway Series meant the world to the two owners and the teams' fan bases. It was George Steinbrenner vs. Fred Wilpon, the Bronx vs. Queens.

In this game, the Mets were clinging to a 1–0 lead. Robin Ventura was on third and shortstop Rey Ordonez was at the plate. Fighting his own hitting woes, he drilled a grounder back to the mound.

El Duque fielded the ball beautifully, but just like Mulholland, he couldn't get the the ball out of his glove. Realizing the ball was stuck, Orlando threw a bullet pass to Tino Martinez at first base! Martinez, seeing that this glove was coming at him full speed, opened his arms and caught it like a wide receiver.

Touchdown, Yankees!

Reggie Goes Yard Again...and Again...and Again

Mr. October certainly earned his nickname in 1977. Game 6 of that season's World Series is one of the most memorable games in baseball history.

Even before Reggie Jackson arrived in the Bronx, he had already achieved individual hero status with the Oakland A's of the early 1970s. From 1972 to 1974, the A's won three straight World Series championships and were an official dynasty, with Reggie front and center.

After all, this was the same guy who hit a home run clear out of the old Tiger Stadium during an All-Star Game. No one but Mickey Mantle hit them that deep, that high, and with that kind of style.

So it was no surprise that when Reggie arrived in New York in 1977, he was on a mission to turn the Yankees into a dynasty.

It was truly the dawning of a new day and a new era for the George Steinbrenner regime. George had bought the team for $10 million back in 1973 and the team floundered. Finding their way in 1976, they made it to the World Series only to lose to the Big Red Machine of Cincinnati. But the Yankees vowed that they'd be hanging around for years to come, and they did.

Billy Martin had brought the same pugnacious attitude to the manager's office that he had when he played for the Yankees way back in the 1950s under Casey Stengel. But with Martin at the helm, was there room for another firebrand? Some said "Maybe," others said "No." George said "Yes!"

Reggie signed a five-year, $3 million deal with the Yankees, big money back then.

The acquisition of Reggie Jackson brought a hoard of media scrutiny and a ton of quotes that I'm sure Reggie would like to forget.

But nothing was going to keep Reggie off center stage in the postseason. Pounded by problems during the season with other players and with Billy Martin, Reggie blocked it all out, as only the great ones can, and made New York his town in October.

Always known for having a flair for the dramatic, whether in print or on the field, Reggie hit three consecutive home runs in that Game 6, each on the first pitch of the at-bat, and each off a different pitcher!

Reggie drew a walk in his first appearance in the second inning, and then he went into home-run mode. He went deep the first time off Burt Hooton, who was known as a crafty guy on the mound, just

Reggie Jackson goes yard three times in Game 6 of the 1977 World Series.

not crafty enough. Reggie then homered on the first pitch he saw from Elias Sosa; both shots landed in the right-field seats.

His final at-bat saw him hit a towering home run off knuckleball legend Charlie Hough. That last jack was such a shot that it landed into the center-field bleachers at Yankee Stadium, reserved only for legends like Ruth, Gehrig, and DiMaggio.

After the night was over, Jackson had gone 3-for-3, with four runs scored, five RBIs, and one walk. Box scores like that make Reggie the one and only Mr. October in my book.

It was Munson who had nicknamed Reggie "Mr. October" in the first place, not out of admiration but out of exasperation. When reporters kept bugging Munson about Reggie's heroics, he kept saying, "Go ask Mr. October." The nickname stuck.

What always amazed me about Reggie was that his swings always looked so good! He didn't have a crazy stance like some hitters do today. He didn't waggle his bat 50 times or adjust his batting gloves between each pitch, driving both the pitchers and the fans nuts. Reggie just stepped in, kept his hands still, and exploded on the ball with a sweet yet violent swing that's impossible to teach.

Mr. October almost single-handedly beat a Dodgers team that many considered to be the favorites in that series. The straw that stirred the drink, indeed.

Bob Feller vs. the Motorcycle

Faster than a speeding bullet! More powerful than a locomotive! No, it's not Superman—it's "Rapid Robert" Feller!

Bob Feller, back in the days before radar guns, took the notion of throwing heat to an entirely new level.

Back then, pitchers didn't know how fast—or slow—they were throwing, and neither did their teams or opposing hitters. Everything was scouted by "feel." Scouts observed pitchers and wrote down very scientific notes like "good arm" or "dead arm." It was rather crude, to say the least. It wasn't as reliable as all the technology we have today, and I'm sure we'll keep refining it until we're satisfied.

There is a lot to be said for modern science. I'm a big believer in the idea that better technology does make for a better life. Lots of old timers like to say, "Back when I played, nobody knew about the disabled list." True, but many great pitchers were sent packing because of injuries that could've been prevented, and in today's game that wouldn't happen. Back then there were no such things as team doctors. The idea of team physicians came well after free agency, well after Curt Flood—bless his soul—forced the owners to stop being so greedy.

Anyway, lots of people thought Bullet Bob Feller was the hardest thrower in the majors in 1940, so one day they decided to put it to the test in the best way they could think of: Feller put his fastball up against a speeding motorcycle!

Here's how they set up the race: a motorcycle was going to drive past Feller at 86 mph, and at that exact moment Bob would uncork his best fastball at a target 60'6" away. You probably guessed how this turned out—Bob's fastball won! The final estimate was his pitch was going 104 mph!

I'm not so sure about 104 mph, but Feller could definitely bring it. The speed guns of today baffle me. When I played, a guy with gas was throwing around 90 mph, but the readings on today's guns are up around 95 or 100. The majority of pitchers are throwing, on average, about 7 to 10 mph faster than they did when I played 15 years ago. But if you try to tell me that guys like Jonathan Broxton of the Rays or Bobby Jenks of the White Sox are throwing harder than Nolan Ryan or Roger Clemens did when I faced them, I'll laugh in your face. Maybe a few guys today are throwing harder than guys did in the late 1980s and early 1990s, but not the majority. So why the discrepancy? Technology. The radar guns today are better. So the pitchers aren't throwing harder, the guns are just better at detecting the actual speed.

I had a strong arm back when I played, but today I can't even throw harder than a slow-moving minivan, so I definitely won't be trying to throw faster than a speeding motorcycle.

Bob should have worn an "S" on his shirt that day, not an Indians logo. If ever there was a Superman on the mound in baseball, Feller gets to throw his name into the discussion.

Willie Mays' Basket Catch

Willie Mays made one of the most memorable catches in baseball history with his famous "basket catch."

But Mays was more than just a guy who made a great catch. We're talking about one of the five greatest players ever! Willie Mays was the epitome of class and dignity. Known for being a down-to-earth guy, he often played stickball in the streets with the kids in Harlem on weekends after games. He was always in shape and always playing at full speed, though he never stole bases just to pad his stats.

Vic Wertz hit a fly ball that seemed to just drift back, and back, and back, until Willie Mays' back was facing home plate. But he never took his eyes off that ball. He stayed with it every step of the way and made an incredible over-the-shoulder basket catch to rob Wertz of a sure double, maybe a triple. But more than that, Mays kept his footing throughout the play. He quickly turned and fired the ball back into the infield and kept the runners on base at bay.

The basket catch is the ultimate Mays moment because he was more concerned about getting the ball back to the infield to hold the runners—the force of which sent him spiraling backward—than he was in showing off after making an incredible catch.

While Mays had done this before, this one came in Game 1 of the 1954 World Series. To this day, Bob Feller calls that catch "tremendous"—and he doesn't say anything nice about anybody.

The Giants used that play to build and hold the momentum that helped them storm through that World Series in a sweep. I wasn't even born yet, so I don't remember anything about that World Series—except Willie's incredible catch.

Willie Mays' classic basket catch—one of the great moments in baseball history.

"The Play"

During the Yankees' most recent run of greatness, it seemed like Derek Jeter was the hero in just about every big win.

Paul O'Neill, Mariano Rivera, Jorge Posada, Andy Pettitte—those guys are true Yankees who epitomize the class and distinction of being part of perhaps the greatest team in sports.

But 2001 was a different beast. New York had a year that started out great and ended horrifically because of 9/11. Game 3 of the 2001 American League Division Series came faster than most would have liked. There was no time to heal.

The city needed a win, needed a reason to smile, and needed Jeter. Jeter, true to his nature, didn't disappoint.

It was the bottom of the seventh, and Oakland, after winning the first two games in the series, was trailing the Yanks 1–0. Not a big deal if they could hold the Yanks down and find a way to score and tie the game.

With two outs, Jeremy Giambi got on base for Oakland. Then Terrence Long stepped up and drove one into the gap. The Yankees' right fielder, Shane Spencer (not sporting his bleach-blonde look that day), picked up the ball and wildly heaved it back toward the infield. I covered that game on TV and was thinking, *Hit the cutoff man.* But this throw was left of the cutoff man and left of the entire field of play. I actually thought it would hit Ramon Hernandez, who was standing in the on-deck circle! Out of nowhere, a full-speed Derek Jeter comes into the picture, and in one motion cuts off the throw and backhands the ball to catcher Jorge Posada at home plate. Giambi, who saw everything unfold before him, was hustling all the way home, but didn't bother to slide when he saw the throw from Spencer was off. He didn't count on Jeter getting to that throw. Nobody did!

I gotta tell ya, being around the game as long as I have, nobody should have been there to cut off that throw. Giambi should have scored standing up with no play at the plate. Jeter shouldn't have been there.

This was a play in a huge game made by a guy who sees things differently than the rest of us. Jeter can see the game in slow motion. He anticipates plays that the rest of the big leaguers might not ever see, and he executes things nobody else would even try.

Can you imagine Jeter ever playing for anyone but the Yankees? Me neither.

Early in his career, the jury was out for me on Derek Jeter. He has never hit 25 home runs. He's only driven in 100 runs once. And yet he's the third-highest paid player in all of baseball. Why?

Well, look at the intangibles. Look at the leadership. Look at the New York police blotter—you won't find him. Look at all those championship rings. The guy just flat out knows the game. You can't teach a lot of the stuff he pulls off on the field. He just has the ability that few players have and the kind of instincts you can't really teach and that you certainly can't replicate.

The Yankees won that game and the next one to send the series to a Game 5 back in New York where they completed their comeback with a third-straight victory. I was able to get a firsthand, up-close view of the site at Ground Zero the day before I called that game. A sight that few got to see and a sight I'll never forget.

I knew, however, that after "The Play," destiny was on New York's side.

Mookie Wilson's Game Winner

Professional baseball players will always tell you they play the game for just one reason: to win a World Series. Nothing else matters, they say, but that's not entirely true. The players get paid a lot of money and, more and more, people have been turned off by the huge sums of money being paid to athletes. Some guys, in every sport, just don't seem all that grateful for their good fortune and they ruin it for the majority of the players who do. If you are one of those fans who believes they're all only in it for the money, let me tell you my story.

Mookie Wilson, Game 6: 'nuff said. Photo courtesy of Getty Images.

When I was three years old, I told my mom I was going to play for the Red Sox. When I was 10, my dad coached my Little League team and he had only one rule: play baseball in the summertime or go on vacation—don't do both. By the time I was in junior high, I played on three different teams, and by high school I was on a team that played 80 games in the summer. While most of my friends went camping or to the movies or just hung out being kids, I was working on my baseball skills. Every weekend, rain or shine, my dad hit fly balls to me. Mother's Day for my mom didn't feature a nice dinner and me cleaning up the kitchen. It was usually my dad pitching, me hitting, and her in center field shagging flies.

Mookie only played 2½ more seasons with the Mets after 1986.

The point is that money never even entered my mind. I played because I loved it; I couldn't get enough of the game. And if you talk to any major leaguer today, you'll hear pretty much the same story from them.

Yes, guys get paid a lot of money, but they can't buy a championship. And that's why winning one feels so good and losing out on one is devastating. Just ask Bobby Thomson and Ralph Branca, or Joe Carter and Mitch Williams. Better yet, let's talk about Mookie Wilson and Bill Buckner. If you're gonna talk about joy and pain, heaven and hell, and the greatest high and the lowest of lows, it's gotta be the 1986 World Series.

I was a member of that Red Sox team in 1986—at least until just before the All-Star break, when I was traded to Chicago for Tom Seaver. The Red Sox and Mets were the teams to beat in their respective leagues and it was the matchup everybody wanted to see. The way the games played out really showed a complete collapse of

Boston's bullpen on a team that really should have won that series. They gave up three runs in the tenth inning of Game 6 to lose it, and then eight runs in the sixth, seventh, and eighth innings of Game 7! But somehow, Bill Buckner took all the blame.

I can tell you that Buckner was one of the most talented, inspiring players I have ever been around. Because of his ankle issues, what he did just to get on the field to play was mind-boggling. The treatment he endured would convince most athletes to call it quits. The guy had a great career, but all anybody wants to acknowledge is that one play.

People forget the scorn that Buckner went through after the World Series was over. He and his family were shamefully run out of Boston, seemingly never to return. But he did return to play in Boston again—twice, both in 1987 and 1990. Now when I see Billy, it seems that all has been forgotten. After all, that was the last World Series game the Red Sox have lost. They've won two titles since and swept the Series each time.

On the other hand, that was probably the greatest night of Mookie Wilson's life. The Mets were down two runs in the tenth with two outs before three straight singles and a wild pitch tied the game. Wilson came up and fouled off pitch after pitch from Bob Stanley, then hit a harmless little bouncer up the first-base line.

When the ball somehow trickled through the legs of Buckner and into right field, the game was over. Mets win.

I've watched the replay of that play 50 times. Buckner didn't miss that ball—it was an act of God. It looked like the ball went through his glove, not under it. Buckner would make that play 100 times out of 100, but not that night. And with that ball went the hopes of a World Series victory that seemed, at the time, like it would never happen for the Red Sox.

Both Wilson and Buckner grew up loving the game, and while they made a lot of money playing baseball, I can tell you neither of them were thinking about how much dough they had in the bank that night. It was all about winning…and losing.

Babe Ruth's Called Shot

History confirms that Babe Ruth pointed toward the bleachers at Wrigley Field in the pivotal third game of the 1932 World Series. But we still don't know what he actually said when he pointed out to the bleachers. Ruth maintained that he called the shot, becoming one of the first athletes to ever "guarantee" a victory.

Today only idiots say stuff like "I guarantee we will win next week's game." It's arrogant, stupid, and a good way to fire up the other team. But think about it. This was a different era, and this was Babe Ruth!

I'd be up for believing Ruth's version of the story because everything we know about the guy makes him seem larger than life to begin with, from his tales of women to his mammoth home runs. To tell you the truth, I'd like to know much more about the Babe's life *off* the field—the record books tell us everything we need to know about what he did *on* the field. Heck, this is a guy who hit more home runs by himself than some of the *teams* he was playing against. There's a reason why, even after all these years, he is recognized as one of the greatest players of all time.

Back then, only the facts of the game got into the papers, not what happened after it. Imagine what would get reported if the Babe was playing today. The media would have killed him. If not the regular beat writers—who seem to write about everything *but* the game these days—then YouTube or TMZ or maybe even *Entertainment Tonight* would find Ruth doing something they deemed inappropriate. They would have questioned his lifestyle and weight and late-night drinking and partying. He would have needed a press agent and a whole team of lawyers fending off frivolous lawsuits and people wanting a handout.

Will we really ever know if Ruth called his shot? Maybe he was pointing at a beer vendor out in the outfield or a pretty girl. Maybe he was just stretching his arms. I choose to believe that he was just so much better than everybody else back then that he could do what no one else could—call his home run shot.

These days, if a guy pointed to the outfield to call a home-run shot, he'd be wearing the next pitch in the earhole of his helmet. But back in the day, guys didn't brawl over nothing and opposing pitchers didn't throw at Babe Ruth.

After all, Ruth saved the game of baseball after the Black Sox scandal, so baseball was more in debt to him than vice versa. I say let the legend live on. This game is all about believing in the things that only our heroes can do.

Eddie Mathews Saves the Day

Doesn't every kid who's ever put on a Little League uniform dream of making the big play that saves the day? Usually that kind of thing only happens in Disney movies, but back in the 1957 World Series, a kid's dream actually came true.

The great Eddie Mathews saved the day to preserve the World Series victory for his Milwaukee Braves against the mighty New York

Yankees. Already a hero after hitting a game-winning home run to put the Braves on top in Game 4, Mathews became a legend after making a great play in Game 7 at Yankee Stadium. Personally, I'd be nervous playing a Game 7 at Yankee Stadium for all the marbles, but Eddie apparently was not. He kept his cool.

The Braves gave Hall of Famer Warren Spahn a five-run lead going into the ninth, but the Yankees rallied and loaded the bases with two outs. In those days, anything could happen at Yankee Stadium; this was back before they renovated the place. You had Death Valley out in left-center field, and if a ball found its way out there, it might roll all the way to the monuments and everybody could score.

But fate rested squarely on the shoulders of Mathews, and he didn't disappoint. Bill "Moose" Skowron hit a sharp grounder to the left side. It appeared at first to be a sure infield hit, but Mathews reacted quickly at third. He moved to his backhand side and snared the ball. Then he ran full speed and tagged third base for the force out. Suddenly the game was over and the Braves were world champions!

One of Mathews' teammates, Frank Torre, was on hand at Shea Stadium in late May 2008 when Joe Torre returned to Gotham for the first time since leaving the Yankees. Besieged by the media, he had a gleam in his eye when we asked him about that play 50 years later.

"It was the greatest moment I had ever had as a player," Frank said, remembering the play as if it happened yesterday. "To be part of a World Series is special, but to win one at Yankee Stadium in enemy territory is beyond belief. I still can't believe Eddie was able to get Moose's shot. It was such a bang-bang play! Eddie grabbed that ball almost behind him and instinctively, in a split second, ran in from behind third base and touched third base and we were World Series champions."

Dancin' on the Wall

Sometimes it takes great effort from more than one player to make things happen in a game. Sort of like when a ball gets smoked in the hole and the shortstop makes an amazing diving effort, gets to his feet, and throws a bullet to first, but the throw is low and the first baseman has to make a great catch to get the out.

On August 5, 2008, during a game between the Red Sox and Royals, there was a play that combined outrageous athletic ability with a crazy balancing act that resulted in a double for Jason Bay.

Bay had just been involved in the Manny Ramirez trade that sent Ramirez to the Dodgers, Bay to the Red Sox, and some minor leaguers to the Pirates. So he was trying to make a good impression on his new teammates and he was off to a great start. He had already made some great defensive plays in left field—something Red Sox fans weren't used to seeing when Ramirez was there—and had a few big hits.

When I was a player, Kansas City still had the AstroTurf playing surface and it was hot in the middle of the summer. I played third base in a game where the temperature on the turf was 142 degrees! I literally had to step into the dirt cutouts around the base so my feet didn't burn between pitches. But the thing I remember most about Kansas City was that the park played big—it seemed like you had to shoot a ball out of a cannon to hit a home run there.

Well, Jason Bay has that kind of power and on that day he absolutely rocketed a ball into deep left-center field. Royals center fielder Mitch Maier raced back on the ball and timed his leap right as he, the ball, and the center-field fence all collided. At first I thought he had caught the ball on a beautifully timed, home-run saving catch, but something caught my eye as Maier was tumbling back to the ground. It was the ball! It had popped out of Maier's glove when he slammed into the wall and it was dancing along the top of the fence, rolling toward left field.

We all know that if the ball falls back into the field of play, it's a fair ball, and if you're Jason Bay, you run as far as you think you can make it. But if the ball happens to roll off the back side of the fence, it's a home run!

Ross Gload was tracking the flight of Bay's blast from his position in left field, giving chase but knowing that Maier had the best chance to make the catch. As Maier smashed into the wall, Gload saw the ball pop out of the glove and start trickling along the top of the wall and he just reacted. The ball had traveled about eight or 10 feet on the wall when Gload jumped up and swatted at the ball with his left hand. His timing was perfect. He kept the ball from going over the fence by knocking it back toward center field. Then he caught his own deflection and threw the ball back into the infield. Bay was safe at second with a stand-up double, but the great play of Maier and the quick thinking by Gload probably saved a home run.

We've all seen balls hit the top of the wall and bounce out for a home run. Even I had two balls bounce out of the gloves of opposing players and go over the fence—in an eight-day span! One glanced off Juan Gonzalez's glove and into the Boston bullpen at Fenway,

Mitch Maier gives it the ol' college try in an effort to rob Jason Bay of a home run.

and a week later I hit one off of Robin Yount's glove and into the same bullpen.

Crazy, I know. It's hard to believe both this play and Kevin Youkilis' ball that landed on the top of the fence at Yankee Stadium both happened in the same season, considering I'd never seen that happen before in my whole life!

The Wizard of Ozzie

Over the years, there have been a few players who have revolutionized their positions. For example, Ozzie Smith and Cal Ripken Jr. did it to the shortstop position in virtually the same era, each in a totally different way. Let me explain. Cal was one of the first big guys to play short with an offensive mindset. He showed bigger guys with bigger bats that they could stay at short and be great players, rather than have to move to third base or to the outfield. That opened the door for guys like Derek Jeter, Alex Rodriguez, and Hanley Ramirez.

Ozzie changed the game at the defensive level. Everybody knows that you better have a pretty sticky guy playing short. It used to be common to refer to a shortstop as "all glove, no bat," so that guy has to be able to catch the ball. But Ozzie took defense to another level with his athleticism and creativity. He tried things on the field that nobody before him would even dare attempt. Because of Ozzie, the new breed of defensive shortstop isn't afraid to make a mistake and can be as creative with his talents as he wants, which brings us to the catch that still sticks in fans' minds 30 years later.

In 1978, Ozzie Smith was playing short for the San Diego Padres, and hadn't yet earned the nickname "Wizard." Ozzie saw a ball hit up the middle to his left by Atlanta Braves star Jeff Burroughs.

Most shortstops would've never even tried to make a play on Burroughs' ball, but the great ones never see a ball that they don't think they can catch. Doubt is never in the mind of a player who is sure of his ability. That's why Ozzie tried to make this play.

Ozzie was a first-ballot Hall of Famer in 2002.

After a few lightning-quick steps, Ozzie began his dive for the ball, fully laid out. But the ball took a weird hop at the end and suddenly the ball was flying over Ozzie's head! That's when Ozzie reached for the stars, caught that ball on the bad hop with his bare hand, got to his feet, and threw Burroughs out at first base!

There are a lot of memorable catches in baseball history, but this play has been a *This Week in Baseball* highlight for 30 years! Heck, it's so memorable that players who weren't even born in 1978 know about that play. Current Dodger Russell Martin is still awed by it, just as kids today are impressed by plays Russell makes as a catcher. Looking out from the dugout with a big smile on his face, pointing to the area between short and second where the play could have happened, Russell shook his head in disbelief when I asked him about it.

"I've never seen anything more dramatic than when I was a kid and saw Ozzie Smith make that play," he said.

Daryl Boston Just Won't Quit

We've all seen great catches in baseball. There are literally hundreds of plays that could be considered—maybe that will be my next book: *Psycho's 100 Greatest Catches.* Hmm….

But every once in a while, you see a catch that you'll never forget, and one of mine was made by Daryl Boston when he was playing left field for the Chicago White Sox.

Daryl was tracking a foul ball down the left-field line in old Comiskey Park, back in the day when ballparks were named for things other than corporations. As the ball continued to drift toward the stands, Daryl didn't hesitate or slow down as he got closer and closer to the cement retaining wall. Running full speed with reckless abandon, it suddenly became clear that he was going to try to catch the ball no matter where it was going to land!

Now, Daryl wasn't some little 5'8" second baseman flipping over the railing trying to make a play and landing in the front row. He's 6'3" and weighed in at about 215 pounds.

So when Boston left his feet, it was the first time I remember being actually fearful for somebody's life

Daryl is now a minor-league instructor for the White Sox.

during a game, but I wasn't sure if I was afraid for Daryl or for the poor fan he was about to land on!

He flew over the retaining wall as if it wasn't even there and dove as far as he could to make the catch. And then, he was gone, literally swallowed up by the crowd!

After a few heart-pounding seconds, everybody quickly began worrying about the safety of both Boston and the fans. But just then Daryl popped back up—in the fourth row of the stands!

Emerging from the crowd and flashing his trademark smile, Daryl lifted is arm and showed everybody that not only was he okay, but he had caught the ball as well!

Those fans at Comiskey Park gave him a standing ovation as he jogged back to the White Sox dugout.

Sure, there are many great catches, but this is one I'll never forget. I'm just glad everybody made it out of there in one piece!

CHAPTER THREE

Wild Kingdom

Randy Johnson's Exploding Bird

At the height of Randy Johnson's most dominant period as a pitcher, nobody wanted to face him. That tailing mid-90s fastball. That ridiculous down-and-in slider. The best hitters in the game found a way to come down with "Johnsonitis" the day he pitched so that they wouldn't have to face him. You've heard of "Johnsonitis," right? It's when a player gets a little tightness in his hamstring—just enough to keep him out of the lineup tonight, but with a little treatment he'll be ready to go tomorrow night—after Johnson has left town.

Jeff Kent holds up one unlucky bird after it was killed by a Randy Johnson fastball in 2001.

Remember the All-Star Game at-bats by lefties John Kruk and Larry Walker? Kruk looked scared stiff standing in there against the Big Unit, and Walker spun his helmet around and switched to the right-handed batter's box. It didn't do either one of them any good, but it did show everybody the feeling you get when you have to face a guy like Johnson in a game that really counts!

So now imagine you're just a little bird, minding your own business. Checkin' into a rumor you heard about a swarm o' bugs making their way down yonder. And if you take a shortcut through the ballfield, you might just catch a good snack for the day before pooping on somebody's shoulder. Unfortunately, somebody forgot to tell you Johnson was pitching that day in a spring-training game. When a 26-ounce bird meets a 97-mph fastball halfway between the pitcher's mound and home plate...nothing but feathers!

Johnson was truly mortified after it happened. He really did feel bad for a long time after the incident. Not that he could do anything about it; that bird had about as much of a chance as Kruk and Walker did of getting a hit, but the timing of that play and the reaction of everybody who saw it makes it one of the craziest baseball plays ever! And I bet word got out to the other birds not to look for any more snacks when the Big Unit is on the mound.

Luis Gonzalez Goes Fishing

We've all hit home runs into fish tanks in our lives, right? Um, not quite!

But Luis Gonzalez can add that to his stellar résumé of things we mortals will never accomplish. Luis had been an exceptional player for the Arizona Diamondbacks, helping them win their first World Series in franchise history in 2001, driving in the winning run against none other than Mr. Lights Out himself, the Yankees' Mariano Rivera.

But this home run with the Dodgers was a bit different. It didn't win a world championship or send the Dodgers to the playoffs.

The mystique of the home run I'm talking about is more about where it landed.

See, the whole fish tank thing happened on June 24, 2007.

It was just another game until the Dodgers' outfielder made a splash during his return to Tampa Bay, a splash in the fish tank out beyond the center-field wall.

Once known by Rays fans for hitting the first home run in Tampa Bay history at the ballpark in 1998 while with the Tigers, Luis gave the St. Pete faithful another home run to remember. The

Go fish! Luis Gonzalez put one in the cownose ray tank at Tropicana Field in 2007.

Rays probably wish they had Gonzalez on their team, since all he does is hit home runs when he visits Tropicana Field.

As I've said numerous times on and off the air, Gonzalez has had a career that any major leaguer would be proud to call his own. Longevity, lots of home runs, tons of doubles, and that little thing called a World Series title.

Tropicana Field is the only stadium in the world that features live rays. Well, duh!

But that's not what this book is about—if you want all his great numbers, go to baseball-reference.com.

During interleague play, the Dodgers had to go down to play the Tampa Bay Devil Rays (now just the Rays). I had never been to Tropicana Field, so I was interested to see all its quirky features—the dreariness of playing indoors, the catwalk above the field that's in play for some reason, plus it was the only ballpark in the big leagues that I hadn't seen.

I was pleasantly surprised. It was brighter than I thought it would be and not at all like the depressing scene that I had heard it was. And the coolest thing they had there was a fish tank full of cownose rays. Deep in the right-field seats, there's a huge tank where fans could come by and pet the rays. I didn't do that, but I could have.

During one of the games, Gonzo pounded a ball into deep right-center and into the tank! I thought, *This has been done before, right?*

We kept our cameras on the ball for a while and the ball just floated there for a bit before sinking.

The rays didn't seem all that bothered to see their home invaded by a baseball. None of them attacked it. None tried to devour it. It was as if this foreign object was under scrutiny by the critters. They didn't know what the heck to make out of it.

Eventually some maintenance worker went out there with a net on a pole and fished it out before the rays could come to a conclusive decision on what to do about it.

In the old days, some stadiums used to have interesting sponsorships like "Hit it here and win a new suit" and stuff like that. They don't do so much of that anymore—at least at the major-league level. I kind of miss that stuff.

I finally got the chance to ask Gonzo if anybody had ever hit the ball into that tank before and he said, "Nope, I hit the first home run in that park and the first one in the tank." I started to wonder if they gave him anything for doing that—a fish dinner somewhere in Tampa would've been nice.

Attack of the Midges

We've seen squirrels, birds, rats, cats, and all sorts of things interfere with play. (Ask the Cubs about goats.) There have been tornadoes and lightning, wind storms, blackouts, but rarely midges. Midges? What the heck is a midge?

I felt for Joba Chamberlain—and the Yankees, believe it or not. "It was the duty of the umpires to call that game," Goose Gossage said after the incident. Goose is right. That game meant way too much to keep playing in under those kinds of conditions. I should know—I played in a game in Cleveland where the exact same thing happened! I had no idea what they were called back when I played for the White Sox and they attacked us at the old Mistake by the Lake. But those bugs that fly in your face, make your neck turn red,

Joba Chamberlain battles the midges and the Cleveland Indians in the 2007 ALDS.

make your eyes itch, and make it impossible to play ball are called midges. Glad to clear it up.

Unfortunately for the young pitcher, Joba Chamberlain didn't stand a chance in Game 2 of the 2007 American League Division Series. There's no question that the game should have been suspended until those little bugs went away, but on they played, and the Indians took full advantage. Joba was so distracted and bothered that he couldn't throw strikes. Cleveland went on to tie the score and eventually won the game in extra innings.

Even Cleveland's Fausto Carmona was affected in the top of the ninth, but not to the same degree as Joba.

"They blew the chance to do the right thing," Gossage said. "I deeply feel baseball suffered a black eye for that bad call. It decided an important series and only the players, in my opinion, should decide a series. Fausto Carmona did not have the intensity of the bugs or the allergic reaction that Joba had. I thought Roger Clemens should have gone to Joe Torre and told Joe to go out and lift him and the team off the field. Joba is young and has guts. He was put in a bad spot. What young kid is going to act like a pussy and asked to be removed? He's not. It was up to the veterans on that team to call timeout and get him and the rest of the guys off that field. Umpires stop games for rain and for fan rudeness, like at Shea when the fans threw batteries on the field. Why not stop the game for this barrage of bugs? This was a bug storm."

Cleveland went on to lose the ALCS to Boston.

Goose was not the type of guy to be rattled by anything back in his heyday, yet he says he would not have been able to pitch under those circumstances.

After all, it's pretty hard to pitch and concentrate when your neck is covered in midges and your face is soaked with bug spray, right in the middle of a critical postseason game on the road in enemy territory. Seems like a lot for anyone to handle, and it seems like the game should have been halted just as games are regularly halted due to fan interference or bad weather.

I'll admit, through it all I had to laugh if only because I had been there before. I knew what Joba and the others were going through, but when I went through it, it wasn't a playoff game with that kind of importance. Heck, when it happened to me, I was with the White Sox—one of the worst teams in the game at that time—playing against a bad Indians team. But I wonder if somewhere along the line, Joba Chamberlain and Ozzie Guillen are related. Nobody that night when I played was more bothered by the midges than Ozzie was. Watching him dance around the infield between pitches, trying to get some relief from the bugs, was almost worth having to deal with them myself. Almost.

Sorry Joba.

Dave Winfield Kills a Seagull

During the 1983 season, Dave Winfield had a lot on his mind.

He and George Steinbrenner were trading insults back and forth in the daily tabloids, a feud that stemmed from a disagreement over Winfield's salary.

What Dave didn't need was to be labeled…a bird killer. Say what? Yep, that's right! Randy Johnson isn't the only guy who's accidentally taken out one of our feathered friends.

During a game in Toronto, Winfield was warming up when one of his throws hit a seagull, killing it instantly. It was an ugly scene, and the fans in attendance immediately started to boo. But Dave wasn't at fault. No player wakes up in the morning and says, "Gee, I think I'll go out and kill a seagull today!" But the fans in Toronto went nuts!

Fans really let him have it that day. Even the environmental groups came out and blasted him. It wasn't as if he'd intended to

A Blue Jays batboy lays a seagull to rest after Dave Winfield accidentally killed it in 1983.

hurt the bird; it was just an accident. But people blamed him and Winfield became the poster child for harming animals. Sometimes it just doesn't pay to get out of bed.

Dave's best defense came courtesy of his manager, Yankee skipper Billy Martin: "They say Winfield hit that bird on purpose. They wouldn't say that if they saw some of the throws he's been making all year!"

A Freaky Friday for Huston Street

Strange things seem to happen when the calendar says Friday the 13th.

In 2008, the Giants were playing the A's in the Bay Area interleague series when Omar Vizquel caught A's lefty Greg Smith napping on the mound in the second inning. Vizquel got a good lead and stole home! It's not too often you get to see a guy steal home, but that was far from the weirdest thing that happened on this Friday.

In the ninth inning, A's closer Huston Street was on the mound to face Fred Lewis with two outs. Huston was all ready to notch another save when all of a sudden, right in the middle of Street's

How refreshing! Huston Street and the A's get soaked by the sprinklers in San Francisco.

windup, the infield sprinklers at San Francisco's AT&T Park went on full blast and soaked Street, Lewis, and all the infielders! The grounds crew said it was a malfunction, but one has to wonder. It was Friday the 13th, after all.

Street went over to shortstop and had a laugh with teammate Bobby Crosby while they waited for the sprinklers to turn off.

"It was the most bizarre thing I had ever witnessed," recalls Mike Sweeney, who was playing for the A's at that time. "I've seen a lot in my years in this game, but I've never seen sprinklers go on in the infield during play and soak the closer during windup before like they did with Huston Street. It was weird."

Hey, it was Friday the 13th. What did Mike expect?

CHAPTER FOUR

Fights, We've Had a Few

Pedro Martinez Body Slams Don Zimmer

Let's see, Fenway Park is known for Fenway Franks, World Series droughts, World Series victories, historic comebacks, Yaz, Teddy Ballgame, Manny being Manny, Psycho (yours truly), Big Papi, Papelbon's *Riverdance*, and....oh yeah, body slams!

Say what?

The craziest thing I've ever seen during a bench-clearing brawl was Pedro Martinez throwing Don Zimmer to the ground at Fenway Park after Zim had come charging at him. Part of me wanted to laugh, which I did. The other part of me was horrified.

The wackiest part of the whole incident was that it took place during the ALCS!

This is the Red Sox–Yankees! These games are supposed to be filled with pitching duels, great defense, home runs, and rabid fans. They are not supposed to look like a WWE pay-per-view!

And any melees are certainly not supposed to involve two guys with an age difference of 40 years. Pedro and Zim going at it was the equivalent of you going after your grandfather if a little scuffle broke out at the family reunion picnic.

Let's go to the tale of the tape in this ultimate showdown: Don Zimmer, 72 years old; Pedro Martinez, 32 years old.

Nice!

Pedro Martinez is a world-class athlete. He's also not afraid to throw inside and hit guys now and then. Just ask Derek Jeter, one of his favorite targets before Pedro moved over to the National League.

Yankees coach Don Zimmer gets to his feet after Boston's Pedro Martinez knocked him down during the 2003 ALCS. Photo courtesy of Getty Images.

Zim, on the other hand, doesn't exactly work out at the gym all that regularly. In fact, I don't know if he's ever worked out a day in the past 25 years.

So let's just say that if Zim was two inches shorter, he'd be round. Pedro, in the all important "reach" category, had Zimmer by about a foot and a half—Zim has alligator arms, for god's sake!

Fair fight? Yeah right!

Hideki Matsui had just busted up a tie game and so Martinez immediately, or "accidentally," threw behind Karim Garcia's head. The home-plate umpire ruled that the ball hit Garcia in the back and issued him a free pass.

Making matters a bit more dicey, the ump then issued warnings to both benches. Alfonso Soriano hit a grounder and Garcia took out Todd Walker hard at second base. When the two rose to their feet, they began scuffling. Now it's on!

All of a sudden this older fat guy comes charging across the field at Pedro. You all know who it is—Don Zimmer!

Martinez, with a quick turn of the body, got poor Zim in a headlock right as Zim was lunging at Pedro, and Pedro just flat-out threw Zim to the ground!

New Yorkers hated Pedro—until he started pitching for the Mets.

Never in my professional baseball or broadcasting career had I seen anything like this.

Both Pedro and Zimmer were extremely embarrassed by the incident—for different reasons, of course.

Zimmer couldn't believe he had charged Martinez and was ashamed that he even tried, and Pedro couldn't believe he became the star of the new reality series *Watch Me Bust Up Gramps!*

I know a lot of people were all over Pedro and I'm sure he feels bad about the whole thing, but what was he supposed to do?

In a brawl you don't look for IDs, and if you see a big guy wearing the other team's uniform flying at you, you put the guy in a headlock and throw him to the ground.

Needless to say, the old Red Sox–Yankees rivalry took on new meaning after that, and little did both teams know that the following year the Sox would beat New York in the greatest comeback in baseball history on Boston's way to a World Series title.

Don't Mess with Nolan

Nolan Ryan is synonymous with no-hitters in my book. I've seen this guy throw no-hitters for so many different teams that it's mind-boggling. I've faced him as a hitter and he's just flat-out scary. He struck fear into the hearts of my teammates before we even stepped into the batter's box. Yet he wasn't a headhunter. He wasn't a mean person. He was just a flamethrower. There's a difference. Nobody ever accused Nolan of throwing at anybody. That was why I was so shocked when he got into the first and only fight of his career. Of all people to fight him, it was Robin Ventura, a nice, mild-mannered guy to boot.

But I guess something bugged Robin, because on August 4, 1993, there was a real, old-fashioned brouhaha in Texas between the Rangers and White Sox.

As a backdrop to the story, it's important to note that at the time Nolan Ryan was at the end of the line as far as his career was concerned. This season was truly his farewell tour, and everywhere Nolan went he was getting standing ovations, even in visiting ballparks.

Ryan was baseball's man of the year in every sense of the word. He was hanging it up and calling it quits to be with his family, and he had fans he never knew existed popping up out of the woodwork on opposing teams—myself included—wishing him well.

Apparently that made no impression on Robin Ventura. I like Robin, but it was a sad sight to see Ventura charge the mound and fight an aging Ryan after Nolan hit him with a pitch.

Kids, always respect your elders: Robin Ventura gets a headlock courtesy of the great Nolan Ryan.

This moment was made doubly psycho because, after getting Ventura in a headlock and not allowing the 26-year-old kid to escape, Ryan gave him a bunch of noogies but was allowed to remain in the game when all was said and done. Gene Lamont, the White Sox manager, got ejected, as did Ventura, but Ryan got to remain in the game. Maybe Nolan had some admirers on the umpiring crew.

Roberto Alomar Gets Spitting Mad

Ever spit in a guy's face and later call him your friend?

September 27, 1996 was a day I'm sure Roberto Alomar wants to forget. That was the day he got into such a heated argument with home-plate umpire John Hirschbeck that Robbie actually bumped him and spit in his face! And I'm talking about a real loogie, not "Oops, I actually got some spittle on you." Alomar reached deep down and got something extra on it.

I've seen Billy Martin kick dirt. I've seen Earl Weaver turn his hat backward. I've seen Tommy Lasorda cuss better than any man should be allowed. But I had never seen a player spit in an umpire's face.

Alomar claims John got personal with him. Hirschbeck claims Alomar brought up the subject of Hirschbeck's child, who was suffering from a rare brain disorder. We'll probably never know the truth, but what we do know is that the incident was so widely televised and talked about that during most of the 1997 season—even after an entire off-season had passed—fans around the league still booed Alomar everywhere he went. He went from being regarded as one of the best second basemen of all time to a guy with questionable character.

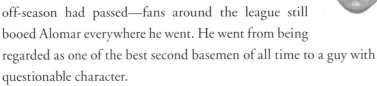

Robbie made 12 straight All-Star teams between 1990 and 2001.

It is ironic how an otherwise meaningless game between the Blue Jays and Orioles turned out to be a turning point in the lives of two good men. But that is exactly what happens when emotions get the better of someone in the heat of the moment.

Roberto Alomar lost his cool and tarnished his legacy after spitting in an umpire's face.

Hirschbeck is a well-respected umpire. He's been around a long time and knows the game well.

Alomar is a Hall of Fame player with some jaw-dropping stats on his resume.

And this is where this story takes a turn for the best.

Most people don't know how hard Alomar tried to reach out to Hirschbeck after the incident. He was ashamed and embarrassed by what he had done and really wanted to make amends.

Hirschbeck, to his credit, listened to what Alomar had to say and felt that his apology was heartfelt and genuine. The two actually became close and worked together on various charity causes. It's an amazing story when two people put a very public lapse in judgment behind them and find the good in one another.

The Mad Hungarian Causes a Brawl

Al Hrabosky was a showman. He's on the all-time list with guys like Mark Fidrych, Bill Lee, and Oil Can Boyd. Al would walk around the mound and pump himself up. He'd get angry and yell at the ball on television. He'd stare down hitters. It was all part of his act. He wasn't just a pitcher, he was an actor on the mound. The baseball field was his ultimate stage. And, of course, he had that mean-looking overgrown Fu Manchu mustache.

Some people understood his act and others didn't. Some liked him, others hated him. In September 1974, Al ran into one of the latter against the Chicago Cubs.

Bill Madlock was one guy who lacked a sense of humor when he was at the plate, and he didn't appreciate all the time Hrabosky took to psych himself up between pitches. Madlock stepped out of the batter's box every time Hrabosky stepped off the mound to do his routine. He'd wait for Al to go through all his shenanigans and then just as Al would get up onto the rubber, Madlock would step out of the batter's box and get some more pine tar for his bat.

Sensing that the crowd was getting restless, home-plate umpire Shag Crawford told Madlock to get into the box and yelled at Hrabosky to pitch.

So Hrabosky did as he was told—he threw a pitch to an empty batter's box because Madlock refused to step in! And then Crawford called it a strike! Madlock was furious. The guy had smoke coming out of his ears; even Hrabosky, now a Cardinals announcer, doesn't deny that.

Jose Cardenal, the on-deck hitter, approached home plate and stepped into the batter's box to join in the argument between Madlock and Crawford.

Much to Al's amazement, there were now suddenly two batters in that tiny batter's box. Then Cubs manager Jim Marshall came charging out and he stood his ground at home plate as well. Poor Al, who just seconds ago had nobody to throw a pitch to, now had three men to throw to.

While the manager, Madlock, Cardenal, and Crawford were continuing their discussion, Hrabosky wound up and threw his next pitch! Of course he drilled somebody—with all those targets, how could he miss?

And yet Hrabosky still has no clue why a brawl started. He still laughs about the whole thing to this day.

"Bill kept stepping in and out of the batter's box and the home-plate umpire yelled at him, 'Get back to the batter's box!' By that time, Shag Crawford told me to throw a pitch," recalls Al. "I threw a pitch with no batter in the batter's box and it really irked Bill. It was the craziest thing I had ever been a part of. The Cubs were furious. They actually sent up two hitters to the batter's box and suddenly, with two guys in the batter's box, and the Cubs manager arguing like a nut, I threw a pitch that hit one of them and it started a bench-clearing brawl. Go figure!"

Johnny Roseboro Attacks Juan Marichal

August 22, 1965, is a day that both Johnny Roseboro and Juan Marichal keep trying to forget. Not to keep stirring the pot, but come on, this moment had to be in the book. After all, not often do we get to to see a hitter, who happens to be the pitcher, take his bat and bludgeon the catcher with it! Who said baseball was all fun and games?

Giants vs. Dodgers is one rivalry in sports that doesn't need its flames fanned. Even in the parking lots at games in L.A. or in San Fran, the fights can get out of hand. I just can't understand the thinking of people who get so psycho over a game that they could ruin the experience for somebody else. It just goes to show you that even in 2009, when tickets cost an arm and a leg, fans still get belligerent just because the guy sitting next to them is wearing the other team's jersey.

In this game, Marichal had knocked down Dodgers legend Maury Wills and Ron Fairly with brushback pitches. Marichal, unlike pitchers today, knew how to throw inside and how to effectively back a guy off the plate. In today's game, pitchers don't practice throwing inside, so they don't know how to do it when they try. And the hitters are so sensitive with their show-me-some-respect attitude that if a pitch gets anywhere near them they want to charge the mound. Sorry, I digress. When Sandy Koufax took the mound for L.A., he refused to retaliate. But Roseboro, his catcher, took matters into his own hands when Marichal came up to bat. After a Koufax pitch, Roseboro's throw back to Sandy came *thisclose* to Juan's face. Marichal didn't hesitate—he turned around and

Johnny Roseboro, meet Juan Marichal's bat.

started beating Roseboro over the head with his bat! It was horrible! Roseboro stood there covered in blood and, of course, the benches cleared and it was on. It took almost 15 minutes to get everybody on both sides to stop the madness.

After the incident Warren Giles, the well-respected NL president, forbade Marichal from participating in games at Dodger Stadium. He was fined but amazingly only got a 10-game suspension.

But it's incredible how time and the bond of athletics can calm even the fiercest of rivalries. The two players actually became friends later in life and appeared in old timers' games and charity events together— almost like teammates.

Marichal's fine was a whopper: $1,750.

I think it would take a lot for me to become friends with a guy who cracked my head open with a baseball bat to the tune of 14 stitches, but crazier things have happened. And I'm counting on it.

Clemens vs. Piazza, Round 1

Roger Clemens, always known for throwing inside, got a little too familiar with Mets superstar Mike Piazza during the summer of 2000. All through the Rocket's career, he had pitched inside. I'm not sure why that's such a big deal to everybody; the great ones all pitched inside. Bob Gibson threw inside. Don Drysdale threw inside. Pedro Martinez throws inside. The philosophy of most successful pitchers is "I'm gonna pitch inside, and if I miss my location, I hope I miss in. And if the guy gets hit, too bad."

During the interleague series at Yankee Stadium in July 2000, Clemens threw a fastball high and inside that hit Mike square in the head. It was a scary sight, but Clemens seemed to not care all that much. Realizing from the throngs of reporters who were concerned about Mike's injuries after the game that this was serious, Roger decided to make a perfunctory phone call to the Mets' locker room. Mike, however, told me he "had nothing to say to Roger." Roger took a beating in the papers for the beanball incident.

But Roger, maybe feeling slighted by the unanswered phone call, was as mad at Piazza as Piazza was mad at him. Of course, there are many, many beanballs every season, and so you may be wondering why this one makes the book.

Stay tuned.

All in the Family

"Doesn't play well with others." Is it possible that Billy Martin's report card had that box checked a few times? Billy was unpredictable, passionate, sometimes drunk, and always lookin' for a fight.

And, as fate would have it, he found a lot of takers.

This particular fight happened on June 18, 1977. The stage was not Zaire, Manila, or Las Vegas; it was Fenway Park.

And Martin didn't get into a ring with just anyone. Rather, he sucker-punched an All-Star on his own team!

Not surprisingly, the incident involved the "straw that stirred the drink" himself, Reggie Jackson. Reggie was playing the outfield and Martin, from his perspective in the dugout cramped into a corner by third base, thought that Jackson didn't hustle on a play in

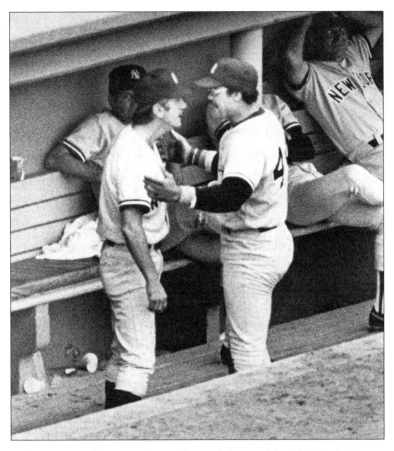

Billy Martin and Reggie Jackson exchange defensive philosophies in the New York dugout.

the outfield. So he decided to take drastic measures: Martin called timeout and pulled Reggie off the field, right in the middle of the inning, on national television.

Jackson couldn't believe it. It was the ultimate embarrassment for a guy who really cared about his image. Upon returning to the dugout, Reggie got in Martin's face and demanded an explanation.

Never known for throwing cold water on a fire, Martin doused the situation with gasoline, exploding on Reggie and getting even more in his face until the two were physically nose to nose. Players and coaches jumped into the fracas and separated the two until Reggie made one remark too many and Martin ran over and threw a punch at him! The two had to be kept at opposite ends of the bench until Martin was taken away into the clubhouse, with Reggie following him a good 20 paces behind.

The Yankees retired Billy's No. 1 jersey in 1986.

If it had been a fair fight, Reggie obviously could have killed Billy. But in an unfair fight, Martin usually had a little advantage. He was used to starting them, and he had a knack for throwing the well-placed sucker punch!

Bill "Spaceman" Lee Fights the Yankees

Bill Lee was nicknamed "Spaceman" for a reason. He drank, smoked dope, and refused to conform to the mainstream. Priding himself on not taking any crap from anybody, Bill often said he'd fight anyone, anywhere.

And on May 20, 1976, he did just that.

Back then, the rivalry between the Yankees and the Red Sox was fierce. Fans today might think the current players dislike each other, but that's nothing compared to the days when Bill Lee was playing.

On this day, a brawl broke out after Lou Piniella ran over Carlton Fisk in a play at the plate. Bill was one of the first guys on the scene, and he separated his shoulder during the melee.

But that was Bill Lee. Bill now lives in the suburbs of New England and enjoys his life. He meditates, regales locals with baseball stories, and does some more meditation. Bill has always marched to his own drum, or tune, or riff, or whatever.

I like Bill Lee because he's an honest guy, and I mean that. There is no BS with Bill. He tells it like it is. If he likes you, he'll let you know. If he thinks you're a capitalist pig out to ruin society, he'll let you know. If he knows you're a Yankees fan trying to disguise yourself as a Sox fan to curry favor with him, he'll punch you out. But seriously, Bill told it like it was back in the day and still does. He's probably one of the most socially aware people out there, but other people's well-being wasn't on his mind during this bench-clearing brawl.

Jeff Nelson Becomes a Bullpen Brawler

We've all heard the saying, "I went to a ballgame last night and a hockey game broke out." Yeah, it's a tired, overused analogy, but you certainly know what the guy's talking about when you hear that: it means a fight broke out on the field or in the stands. And when those kinds of things happen in a playoff game, everybody knows about it.

There are more than a few stories in this book involving the fierce rivalry between the Yankees and the Red Sox, and after playing each other 19 times during the regular season in 2003, you expected there to be some fireworks when they met up again in the postseason. But did anyone expect fights, arrests, and lawsuits?

Game 3 of the ALCS was the marquee matchup everybody wanted to see, with the series knotted at one game apiece: Pedro Martinez vs. Roger Clemens.

Just thinking about it makes me want to watch a replay of that game. But things got ugly that afternoon both on the field and…in the bullpen? I'll explain.

> Jeff still holds the Mariners record for most games pitched (432).

It started off with a brief bench-clearing incident in the fourth inning. I don't think I'd call it a brawl—more of a discussion between the two teams. Karim Garcia got plunked in the back by Pedro and so the next inning, Clemens threw his patented "bow tie" pitch up and in to Manny Ramirez. Manny didn't appreciate it and came out toward the mound to deliver his complaint personally.

I'd say about 90 percent of baseball "fights" are like that. Fifty players end up on the field and everybody acts like they want to fight with someone, but it's really just a big dance-off. And if there's a player, coach, or umpire between the guy who's acting like he wants to fight and his target, he puffs his chest out even more, knowing that nothing will happen. All it really does is pump up the crowd a little and give the announcers something to talk about.

Both teams settled down and the Yankees took a 4–3 lead into the ninth inning, though most people only remember what happened then down in the Yankees' bullpen. I've often talked about how players really have to restrain themselves when they have a uniform on. Fans can say some really nasty things to players, but the players know they just have to let it all go in one ear and out the other. Guys get yelled at, spit on, gestured to, and sometimes even have objects thrown at them. They have to endure the fans—usually the ones who have had too many beers—who think it's cool to berate and belittle guys who are just trying to do their jobs. But does a player have to show the same restraint when the person abusing him isn't a fan, but is actually an *employee* of the other team? I guess I would say yes, but everybody has their limits. Jeff Nelson got pushed past his.

Nelson decided he had heard enough from a guy who was waving a Red Sox rally towel and acting like a jerk. Nelson told the guy to knock it off. When the guy didn't, Nelson decided to go shut him up personally. But he didn't have to go into the seats to do it. The guy who was causing all the trouble worked for the Red Sox grounds crew! He was assigned to the Yankee bullpen and thought it would be okay to harass the Yankee relievers like he was Joe Sox Fan.

Nelson grabbed him by the shirt and they wrestled each other to the ground, where Nelson threw a few haymakers. Then Karim Garcia, the Yankees' right fielder, came running over and joined the fight, as did a few other members of the bullpen just for good measure.

The part-time Red Sox employee who ended up being the punching bag, Paul Williams, was a special-education teacher in New Hampshire. He had to go to the hospital to be treated for his injuries and left the next day wearing a neck brace—lawsuit to follow.

Garcia injured his hand, presumably on Williams' face, and was questionable for Game 4, though he did play. For their parts in the mess, Nelson and Garcia were charged with assault and battery;

Williams was relieved of his duties pushing dirt around at Fenway. Years later I asked Joe Torre if anything came of the charges or the lawsuit. He said he didn't know of any serious action taken by either party, and that both sides were at fault.

Nelson is a guy everybody should remember, and not for what happened that day in Boston. He played for 15 years in the big leagues, won four world championships with the Yankees, and is second on the all-time postseason appearance list with 55, behind only Mariano Rivera.

It amazes me how many of the stories I've written about in this book actually happened in games that are the most important—playoff games, World Series games, and All-Star Games.

Maybe the biggest stage and the pressure to win those big games brings out the worst in all of us when we're hoping for the best. There's no question it brings out our psycho side.

Pete Rose Clocks Bud Harrelson

Someone should have told Pete Rose that the NLCS is not the best place for starting a brawl. But Charlie Hustle only knew how to play the game one way—by giving 100 percent at all times, no matter what.

And Rose certainly gave fans at Shea Stadium their money's worth during the 1973 postseason series between the Reds and Mets. Jerry Koosman was on the mound for the Mets that day and his offense scored nine times in the first four innings. Ouch! I guess that was when Rose decided to take his frustration out on somebody, only instead of getting payback at the plate against Koosman, he went after Mets shortstop Bud Harrelson.

Stay classy, Pete: Rose pops up and punches Bud Harrelson during the 1973 NLCS.

When Rose barreled into Buddy on a routine play in the fifth inning, it caused quite a melee as both benches emptied. Rose and Harrelson punched themselves silly; it was definitely one of the better fights of all time.

Usually when the bullpens empty in a fight, nothing really happens. But not this time! Pedro Borbon and Mets pitcher Buzz Capra went at it, and when I say they went at it I mean they really made a beeline for one another. And then things got even crazier as Duffy Dyer slugged Borbon! Even the fans got into the act—big surprise, being in New York—and threw everything they had on the field, from hot dog wrappers to whiskey bottles.

The Mets literally had to plead with their fans to calm down so the game wouldn't be forfeited. A playoff game! When it was all over, Borbon found himself wearing a Mets cap. When somebody finally noticed it and brought it to his attention, he took a bite out of it!

Clemens v. Piazza, Round 2

The 2000 World Series was the matchup that all of New York wanted to see and the rest of the country dreaded: the mighty Yankees vs. the underdog Mets.

Considering all the hype that goes into any Series, plus the fact that the entire thing was happening in New York City, the media couldn't help themselves—everyone wanted to keep the controversy going between Roger Clemens and Mike Piazza. Clemens told me that he had forgotten the whole thing—it was just another play that had happened months ago during the regular season. He threw inside, it got away from him, and Piazza got hit. End of story.

Well, maybe it was over in his mind, but the whole country was getting geared up for the first showdown between the greatest power pitcher of my generation vs. the greatest hitting catcher who ever lived. Get a good seat, Act II was about to begin.

When Clemens pitched, he was in another world. After playing with him and observing him from the booth for all those years, I got the feeling that his focus was always more on the individual battle being played out between himself and the hitter rather than on the game as a whole. His level of concentration was legendary. I believe he rarely cared who was actually in the batter's box and was just concerned with getting the guy out.

As Piazza strolled to the plate in Game 2, the place was electric. When Clemens peered over the top of his glove to get the sign, there was little doubt about which pitch he was going to throw. Clemens had many weapons he could use. If he had to trick a hitter or outsmart them, he had an excellent breaking ball and would also use a splitfinger at times. But this wasn't about fooling anybody. Not this hitter. Not this time. Not Piazza. This was about power vs. power and everybody in the stadium and watching at home knew what was coming—fastball!

There was a bit of confusion after Rocket's pitch shattered Piazza's bat and pieces of it started hurtling their way toward Clemens. Where was the ball? Why was Piazza running down the line? As it turned out, Piazza's mighty swing had produced a little dribbler down the first-base line, foul, but a big piece of his bat was headed right at Clemens' feet. Roger quickly sidestepped to his left and made a great play fielding the business half of Piazza's Louisville Slugger. Then something crazy happened, and to this day it's never been adequately explained: Clemens turned and then let loose, throwing the bat right at Piazza!

Mike had to sidestep the jagged edge of his own bat while on his way to first base. When he realized what Roger had done, he wasn't too happy about it, motioning toward Clemens and making his way toward the mound.

Clemens was moving toward the first-base line and the two met briefly and exchanged words. Luckily, the situation never developed much further and things quieted down from that point. I think most players thought Mike had every right to clock Clemens right then and there, but Piazza took the high road.

Roger Clemens throws a broken bat at Mike Piazza—I mean, back toward the dugout—during the 2000 World Series. Photo courtesy of Getty Images.

That was one of the most bush-league plays I have ever seen. The funny thing was that Clemens wanted no part of Piazza once Mike started walking toward the mound. He talked the talk but didn't walk the walk.

Think about it: you're in the World Series, on national TV, and you try and injure the other team's marquee player—and it was the same guy you had already hit in the head during the season! Everyone who saw that play has their own take on what the hell Clemens was thinking. I don't buy Rocket's defense that he was just angry at himself and was throwing the piece of wood back toward the batboys near the dugout, but I do believe what he said about fielding the bat originally. He thought it was the ball. When something comes flying at you as a baseball player, you react and make the play. Nobody would try to catch a flying bat if he knew that's what it was. But throwing the bat is harder to swallow.

Even after everything that Clemens has been through, I still love the guy. He was quite simply the most talented, hardest-working, and toughest competitor I've ever seen. That's still worth something to me. The steroid allegations and his damaged reputations are issues that he has to deal with personally. As far as getting the true story on why he threw that bat at Piazza? I guess we'll have to wait for his book.

I have never seen anything that psychotic during a World Series. It changed the complexion of the series and kind of marred it for most people who are true die-hard baseball fans.

CHAPTER FIVE

That's Incredible!

Turning a Triple Play...Without Touching the Ball!

I'm not usually very good at baseball trivia because I'm not a great historian of the game. That kind of stuff rarely sticks in my brain, so if you've got a trivia question for me, I probably don't have the answer.

But I *do* have one trivia question I stump people with all the time: "Can you name the last American League switch-hitter to win the MVP Award?"

The answer, of course, is Vida Blue. He was a pitcher (but you knew that) and he just happened to switch-hit as well.

Now here's a play that happened in a minor-league game that nobody would believe was possible if they weren't there to see it. But Buck Showalter was, as the manager of one of the teams involved, and he told me the whole story.

The opposing team turned an unassisted triple play without ever touching the ball.

Yeah, go back and reread that to make sure you've got it right.

Now, put this book down and try to imagine any scenario where that could happen. It might take a while, and you'll really have to stretch your imagination to come up with anything close.

Here's the story:

Obviously, we start with guys on base—you can't turn a triple play without base runners. In this case, the runners were on first and second. Then it gets really weird.

With no outs and a 3–2 count on the hitter, both runners took off to attempt a double steal. "That was my first mistake," Buck said. "If you watch any game I've ever been involved with since that day, you know I will never send the runners in that situation ever again—but I was young and thought I knew everything, so…."

I've always thought that's a bad play because with no outs the hitter can hit into a fairly easy triple play if he hits a line drive to any of the infielders. But remember, on this play, the defense doesn't even touch the ball!

As the runners took off, the hitter popped one up in the infield. The umpires correctly called the "infield fly" rule, so the batter was out. So now you've got one out, right? The base runners should've gone back to tag up, but this game was during what they call "extended spring training," a place where the players are either young and don't know what they're doing or are about to get released because they're old and don't know what they're doing.

There have been fewer than 700 triple plays turned in the history of Major League Baseball.

The runner from second base did go back to tag up, but the runner from first didn't. He didn't bother to see where the ball was hit, he didn't pick up Showalter coaching at third base, he didn't see anything—he just kept going! So when he eventually rounded second base, he passed the runner who was originally on second base trying to tag up. Now the runner from first was out, and that made two down.

What else could possibly happen? It's already a crazy play that would have any manager pulling his hair out.

Well, the runner on second base was so busy trying to get back to second, he forgot to track the ball in the air and he actually got hit with the batted ball—triple play!

Think about how long it would take for the umpires and players to sort this whole mess out. You gotta think everybody was just kind of standing around saying, "What just happened?" Yeah, me too. Triple plays happen—not all that often, but they do. But this is the only play I've ever heard of where the defensive team never even touched the ball and therefore no assists were made on the play.

After Buck filed his daily report with the Yankees organization, the minor-league director called and asked him to explain the play one more time. Hoyt Wilhelm, who had been around the game of baseball for more years than all of the guys involved in that play put together, saw it all happen. Hoyt spent the day sitting in a lawn chair behind home plate, charting the pitchers from his comfortable perch, and he actually got up from his chair and came all the way over to the dugout to say, "I ain't never seen nothin' like that before," then went back and sat down. The umpire even came up to Buck the next day and asked, "Does stuff like that happen all the time?"

Beyond crazy.

Darren Baker's Close Call

For some reason, a lot of the craziest plays ever recorded seem to have happened in the playoffs or World Series. You'd think by that point in the season, both teams would have everything down cold and the wackiness would be at a minimum, but that's not always the case.

For example, consider Game 5 of the 2002 World Series. Dusty Baker was managing the NL champion San Francisco Giants and he was trying to win their first World Series in nearly 50 years. The last time the team won was back when they were the New York Giants in 1954. The Angels were trying to make some history of their own by winning the first championship in franchise history.

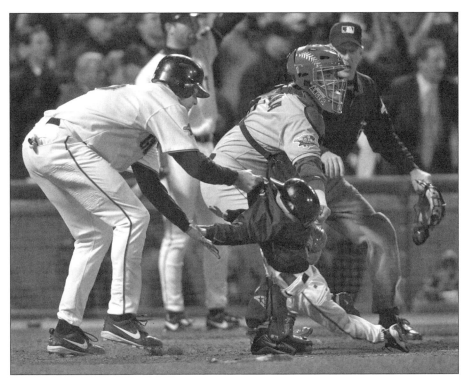

Now this is how you impress your manager! J. T. Snow saves Dusty Baker's son from getting trampled in 2002.

What nobody expected was that the batboy, who just happened to be Dusty Baker's son, Darren, would get in harm's way.

Darren was excited to be there. Dusty is famous for wanting the sons of his players to be around his team all the time. He wanted to keep the father-son relationship strong and emphasized the importance of family to his players.

Dusty told me that every kid would get assigned one player to be responsible for and would become their own personal batboy. Darren loved Kenny Lofton; he was his favorite player and was always assigned to get Kenny's bat. There was no way Darren would let anybody else get Lofton's bat.

As the game wore on, one of the other kids was teasing Darren and told him that he was going to get Lofton's bat after his next at-bat. Darren wasn't going to let that happen, so as soon as Lofton made contact, Darren darted from the dugout and went after that bat.

The only problem was that while Darren was racing toward home plate, J.T. Snow was barreling around third and on his way home—and teammate David Bell was right behind him. Snow was easily safe at the plate and had a second or two to assess the situation, so when he saw Darren standing too close to home plate, he literally scooped up Darren by his jacket and pulled him to safety. A split second later, Bell came flying home.

Dusty took over the Reds in 2008, and Darren is still right there with him.

It took a few seconds for everybody to realize what had just happened. What was J.T. doing and who was that little kid he was holding?

The incident is funny only because no one got hurt, but the point wasn't lost on Baker's mother, Christina, who called Dusty in his office to chastise him for not supervising her grandson. When I asked Dusty what the first thing he thought of was when he saw what was happening, he said, "My mom." She had previously warned her son that the kid might get hurt being out there and, as usual, Mom was right!

Snow was always regarded as one of the best defensive first basemen in baseball, and on that night he made one of his best "picks" ever!

Carlton Fisk Tags Two Yankees

As far as base running is concerned, August 2, 1985, was one of the weirdest days in baseball history.

This was the day that George Steinbrenner, who always takes bad plays in stride—yeah, right!—saw two of his better players get tagged out at home plate *on the same play* by Chicago's Carlton Fisk!

At the time, Dale Berra was a solid player. He had learned the game from his legendary father, Yogi, and played hard. Bobby Meacham also maximized his talent and played the game the right way. Both men were known as competitors on the field. So it was surprising that both would be involved in a play that was bad from start to finish. But thanks to them, we've got a great story that will live on forever in Yankee lore.

Dale Berra was on first, Bobby Meacham was on second, and Rickey Henderson was up at the plate. Henderson hit a rope to left-center field. Meacham, however, thought that the ball was going to be caught. He decided to remain at second, tagging up so he could advance to third. Berra, however, had a different idea. He ran full-speed ahead and almost passed Meacham! Meacham, seeing the speeding Berra out of the corner of his eye, took off for third without tagging, but he stumbled along the way. The two reached third at about the same time. This caused Gene Michael, the Yankees' third-base coach, to throw his hands up in the air in disbelief. Not knowing what to do then, both runners kept going and headed for home! This is where the fun began.

Carlton Fisk took a relay throw from Ozzie Guillen and tagged both men out one after the other. It was awesome because Fisk had to first tag Meacham on one side of the plate and then have the presence of mind to reach back to the other side to get Berra. You don't see the Yankee Stadium crowd in disbelief very often, but this play had the entire place in stunned silence. Both guys out at home on the same play!

Fisk is second on the all-time home run list for catchers behind Mike Piazza.

The play was pretty comical to everyone except George Steinbrenner. After all, this was the man who had a a secretary fired for ordering the wrong sandwich!

At that time, George wasn't mellow, and he had trouble taking nutty plays like this one in stride, but he did forgive in the end. Lucky for Berra and Meacham.

The Pine Tar Incident

George Brett once said that he liked to watch *The Rockford Files* on television. For those born after 1970, Brett was referring to a show now seen in reruns. It was a classic detective mystery series starring James Garner. I think, in tribute to Brett, they ought to have made an episode on the pine tar game, as it was one big mystery to me.

It happened on July 24, 1983, at Yankee Stadium. Billy Martin had just returned to the helm at the Bronx Zoo. George Brett was tearing up the league at the time, batting close to .360.

Goose Gossage had come on in the late innings and was pitching for the save in the top of the ninth. Brett was up at the plate and…

boom! He hit a monster home run off Gossage and the Royals took the lead 5–4.

Billy, always in the mood for a tussle, ran out to home plate after Brett hit the home run and started hooting and hollering at the umpires. Martin told them that pine tar couldn't be applied more than 18 inches up the handle of the bat.

Okay…so what?

Well, Tim McClelland, the home-plate umpire, agreed to measure the pine tar on Brett's bat. He laid the bat across home plate (which measures 17 inches wide) to see just how far up the handle Brett had applied the pine tar. Turns out it was up around 24 inches.

McClelland then conferred with the other umpires. After the huddle was over, he approached the Royals' dugout and motioned that Brett was out!

George Brett charged out of that dugout like a mad bull. He had to be restrained by his teammates and other umpires for fear that he might cause bodily harm to McClelland.

I wouldn't have wanted to be the guy who told George Brett that he had too much pine tar on his bat and that it was too far up the bat barrel to boot, but Billy Martin didn't care. Ironically, Martin just stood there, calm as could be. That's coming from a guy who once told Goose Gossage to hit Billy Sample in the head during a spring-training game, which Goose refused to do and which ultimately got Goose booked into Martin's doghouse. Billy loved confrontation and he certainly irked Brett with this move. The game ended up being halted and then finished some weeks later after the Royals appealed to the league office. It was ultimately decided that McClelland had ruled incorrectly and the Royals ended up winning on the strength of Brett's home run.

George Brett politely disagrees with umpires in the infamous pine tar incident.
Photo courtesy of Getty Images.

Martin was right about the rule—it states that you cannot have pine tar more than 18 inches up the handle of your bat. But if the opposing team wants to challenge a player, they must do it *prior* to the at-bat in question.

But thanks to Billy (God rest his soul), we got a story baseball fans will remember forever.

No Use for This Glove

He was an MVP. He has also been shot three times. He once showed up to spring training 30 pounds heavier—not from working out or using steroids, but from eating too much that off-season. Some say he once killed a cat on purpose; others say he punched a minor-league owner in the mouth during a brawl. He played in Japan, he's a former gang member, he's got a World Series ring, and he even managed a team after his playing days were over.

It's been said about a select few that they "did it all," but when you look at this guy's résumé, it might be the truth.

Who is he?

Kevin Mitchell.

Mitchell was so gifted as a young player that Gary Carter used to call him "World" because there wasn't a place on the field he couldn't play. His career was dotted with both greatness and events that everybody just scratched their heads over. He's still the only MVP to bounce around to eight different teams during his career and play in Japan.

The 1986 season was a crazy one for a lot of people. I played on the Red Sox team that was beaten by the New York Mets for the World Series title when that infamous ground ball trickled through Bill Buckner's legs. Many people like to forget that the Buckner play actually happened in Game 6 and that the Red Sox had a chance to win Game 7 two nights later—but it didn't happen.

Mitchell was a big part of that Game 6 comeback victory, but rumor has it he was in the clubhouse, halfway out of his uniform, making travel plans to go home when they were looking for him to pinch-hit. They found him, he got a hit, and eventually he scored the tying run of that game on the way to a stunning Mets win.

Mitchell has disputed claims by Dwight Gooden that he decapitated his girlfriend's cat in the heat of a domestic dispute. Clearly, Mitchell and Gooden got to the point where they weren't seeing eye to eye on things.

Even though Kevin had already established himself as a successful big leaguer, his big season happened with San Francisco in 1989—the same season he made a play that to this day defies explanation.

> Kevin ended his career with 234 homers; he could've hit a lot more.

Mitchell and the Giants were playing in St. Louis. With the great Ozzie Smith at the plate, Mitchell was in left field, playing a little shallow and shaded toward the left-field line. But Ozzie connected on a ball and hit it a little farther than Mitchell expected, which meant Kevin really had to get on his horse to try and track it down. He was running full speed into the left-field corner of Busch Stadium and he definitely had a great shot at making the catch. But for some reason, instead of sticking his glove up, he reached up with his right hand and made the catch *bare-handed*!

I never heard Mitchell give a legit reason for why he used his meat hand instead of his glove, and I certainly can't think of any reason I would do it either. He just reacted to the ball and for some reason his brain told him to use the wrong hand. It all worked out and he made a catch that is still on the highlight reels to this very day. That was just one of the memorable moments for Mitchell in 1989—he went on to have by far the best year of his career, earning MVP honors for the huge numbers he threw up: a league-leading 47 home runs and

125 RBIs. He never came close to duplicating those numbers again, and as far as I know, he never tried to duplicate that catch!

Eck and the Earthquake

When the heroic closer trots in from the bullpen with the crowd on its feet, or when the hometown favorite ropes a home run to win a ballgame, broadcasters sometimes tell viewers that the "ground is shaking" to describe the intensity of the moment. Most of the time that announcer is just trying to convey the drama.

But in 1989, during the World Series between the A's and Giants, the stadium actually *did* shake, and the real thing was far more dramatic than anything that could ever happen on the diamond.

A major earthquake actually rocked the entire city of San Francisco. It has since been declared one of the worst in the city's history, destroying bridges, killing people, and causing damage to homes and businesses that took a decade to overcome.

The fact that it was the first-ever all–Bay Area series and that the A's became the first team in 13 years to sweep took a backseat to the real headline. The huge earthquake that shook the city caused a 10-day halt to the World Series. But the lives of those devastated by the earthquake did not resume. People lost their homes, their possessions, their lives, and their loved ones.

A's closer Dennis Eckersley was in the men's room when it all went down. Imagine being in the bathroom during an earthquake!

"I knew it the second it happened," Dennis recalls. "It was like a train coming through the door. I was in the bathroom and I just got the hell out.

"I still remember the locker room in old Candlestick Park being right near the parking lot and I just bolted. I was out in about 10 giant steps. The weird thing was that while this was all happening, they were playing the song 'We Will Rock You' and the crowds were either stupefied or they were in party mode because they were not taking it all too seriously. Obviously, the next day, when we took four hours to get to Oakland because the Bay Bridge went down, the atmosphere in the stands was solemn and extremely out of sorts. It was a tragic event that caused devastation."

The World Series is the pinnacle of a ballplayer's career, but the anticipation and excitement were drowned out by the panic and tragedy caused by the earthquake. A's catcher Terry Steinbeck summed up the feelings of a lot of people when he said, "We won, but with all that has happened, I don't even care."

Manny Ramirez High-Fives a Fan and Turns a Double Play

Most of the time, "Manny being Manny" isn't a good thing.

When Manny Ramirez was with the Red Sox, "being Manny" usually meant doing something stupid or selfish. Cutting off throws from the outfield, faking injuries, and not hustling down the line on ground balls were just some of the things that Red Sox management had to endure. There was no question that by 2008, both sides wanted out of the marriage. But a lot of the time, Manny was just being a big kid playing the high-stakes game of Major League Baseball. Ramirez is among the highest-paid players ever, but he plays with a boyish charm and grin on his face. He is a tireless worker and often includes his teammates in his joy, working out different handshakes for different friends and genuinely rooting for the other guys on his team. I've never seen a player include his teammates in celebrations the way Manny does. High fives, chest bumps, smiles everywhere—Manny makes every guy on the team feel like he hit the home run himself.

There's no question that he is one of the smartest hitters of this or any generation—almost like a hitting savant with a game plan that he rarely varies from. Few people would call him an excellent overall baseball player, but nobody would deny that he is one of the most feared hitters ever and will be a first-ballot Hall of Famer.

Manny hit 274 home runs as a member of the Red Sox.

On May 14, 2008, Manny was definitely being Manny.

I couldn't believe it when it happened and came across the wire. Only Manny Ramirez, in a visiting stadium, could make an over-the-shoulder catch against the wall, jump up to high-five a Red Sox fan who happened to be sitting there, and then fire the ball back in to help turn a double play.

The Sox were playing the Orioles in Baltimore. Kevin Millar hit a towering drive to left. Manny raced back and made a leaping catch near the warning track. Seeing Manny go back on the ball perfectly and make the play the way a good left fielder should was probably enough for most Red Sox fans, but just making the catch wasn't enough for Manny. Ramirez jumped up on the wall and reached over to high-five a Red Sox fan wearing a Red Sox jersey in the front row, and then fired the ball into second base that was relayed to first to turn the double play! Millar was stunned. Heck, Manny's own teammates were stunned!

Manny being Manny, this time high-fiving a fan before starting a double play in Baltimore.

I'm not too sure why any of the Red Sox would be amazed—they had watched Manny do crazy things for years. Remember when he took an iPod out to the left field with him? Or the time he made a cell phone call while the Red Sox were making a pitching change? He once ran out carrying an American flag—that was cool because he had just become an American citizen. Another time he was late getting back on the field after retreating into the left-field scoreboard at Fenway during a pitching change. Some say he was taking a whiz; others say he was just hangin' out with the scoreboard operators. Either way, somebody had to stop the pitcher from pitching until they could get Manny back into position. Manny being Manny....

Reggie's Rear Gets in the Way

As if Reggie Jackson hadn't irked the Dodgers enough with his three home runs in Game 6 of the 1977 World Series, he came back for more in the Dodgers-Yankees rematch in 1978.

A packed house of fans in Yankee Stadium was waiting to explode—what else is new?—in Game 4. Ed Figueroa and Tommy John were battling each other in a scoreless game until the Dodgers struck hard in the top of the fifth, scoring three times.

In the bottom of the sixth, Reggie put some wood on the ball and got on base with a one-out RBI single. With Reggie on first base and Thurman Munson at second, Lou Piniella hit a soft liner that Dodgers shortstop Bill Russell dropped. Maybe he dropped it on purpose to try and turn a double play, because he quickly stepped on second base and threw to first for what should have been an inning-ending double play.

But come on, these are the Dodgers and Yankees playing! Something weird had to happen! Sure enough, Russell's throw struck Jackson in the hip and the ball bounced off Reggie and into foul territory. Steve Garvey, the first baseman, ran over to yell at the first-base umpire, forgetting that the play had not been called dead, allowing Munson to run all the way around from second to score.

"He was out of the base path," claims Dodgers great Rick Monday to this very day, and Rick was there, front and center!

Reggie knew he was going to be out, so he positioned himself in the way of Russell's throw. When the throw was made, Reggie realized that it wasn't going to hit him so he threw his hip out and made *sure* it hit him. Reggie was called safe and the Dodgers went nuts!

The umpires tried to explain to Dodgers manager Tommy Lasorda that Reggie's play was legal. That didn't go over too well with Lasorda, who reminded the umpires he knew some not-fit-for-print words that Merriam-Webster don't include in their dictionary.

The Dodgers' protests fell upon deaf ears. The Yankees tied the game in the bottom of the eighth and Reggie and company came back to win the game in the tenth, highlighted by Reggie's singling of Roy White over to second followed by a game-winning single courtesy of Piniella.

I'm sure if there was one guy that Tommy Lasorda wished he had never had to manage against, it may well have been Reggie Jackson. The guy just killed the Dodgers. When he wasn't beating them at the plate, he was stretching the rules and beating them on the base paths.

I remember watching it all on television and thinking to myself, *Only Reggie can pull this off.* And only Mr. October could do it in the World Series.

The Longest Single

I was always a rah-rah guy. I got excited about the game and loved it when my teammates did something well. I was always the first guy on the top step to congratulate someone after a home run and the first guy giving out the high fives after a good play. I guess that made me a highly paid cheerleader, especially when I wasn't actually playing that day—which happened a lot! But you can take that stuff too far. If you do it the wrong way or at the wrong time, it's called "showing up" the other team. There's a fine line between exuberance and pissing off your opponents. And whatever you do, don't ever, under any circumstances, let your joy for the game and your own personal happiness affect the outcome of a game.

Of course, it's happened before. Here's a good rule of thumb on home-run etiquette: always wait for the guy who hit the home run to touch home plate *before* you start congratulating him, jumping on him, and giving him a high five.

I wish someone had told Todd Pratt about my cardinal rule back in 1999 during the NLCS between his Mets and the Braves.

The Braves had been the team of the decade in the 1990s and while they won just one World Series, they had claimed eight straight division titles. (They would go on to win 14 straight.) The Braves beat the Mets and then went on to lose to the Yankees in the World Series, but that postseason is remembered by many because of the infamous Robin Ventura single, a play that actually should have been a game-winning grand slam.

It was Game 5, top of the fifteenth inning. Yes, I said the *fifteenth*. The Mets and Braves were knotted at 2–2. Mets reliever

Mets catcher Todd Pratt celebrates with Robin Ventura…and costs his teammate a grand slam. Photo courtesy of Getty Images.

Octavio Dotel gave up an RBI triple to Keith Lockhart, and Atlanta took a 3–2 lead heading into the bottom of the fifteenth.

The Mets found a way to load the bases against Braves reliever Kevin McGlinchy. It was now up to Robin Ventura, the man who hit 18 grand slams in his career, which is fourth on the all-time list.

Robin is one of only five third basemen with 250 career homers and five Gold Gloves.

Remember, the Mets needed to win in order to extend the series to a Game 6. This was one of those pressure-packed moments that every player dreams about. Ventura, as he had done so many times before, got a pitch he liked and drove it deep into right-center field for a home run! Add another granny to Ventura's lifetime list…right?

Enter Todd Pratt, the Mets catcher who was on first base after having drawn a walk to tie the score. He had a great view of Ventura's shot leaving the park. Todd's emotions took over, so he just stood there between first and second jumping up and down and waiting for Ventura to catch up to him. When he did, Pratt almost tackled Ventura, spinning him around in a bear hug as the rest of the Mets began to converge on the celebrating duo. But when Pratt spun Robin around, technically Robin passed Pratt on the base path, so he was called out!

The runner on third scored and the Mets won the game, but Ventura got credited with a single and *not* a grand slam.

I guess you'd have to call Pratt a rah-rah guy, too. I'm not sure what Ventura calls him.

Cleveland's Triple Steal

Just when you think you've seen it all, another nutty play comes along. This one came courtesy of the Cleveland Indians and is so far-fetched it could've been in the movie *Major League*.

In an otherwise ordinary victory over the White Sox on May 27, 2008, the Indians actually pulled off a triple steal.

Cleveland had David Dellucci on third, Grady Sizemore on second, and Jamey Carroll on first, with Ben Francisco at the plate. But on this play, all Ben had to do was stand there and watch.

First, White Sox pitcher Ehren Wasserman decided to do the old fake-to-third-but-throw-to-first move. The move caught Carroll off guard and off base, but first baseman Paul Konerko botched the rundown and then things deteriorated fast for Chicago.

Dellucci took off for home from third because Konerko was trying to figure out how to chase down Carroll and tag him out. Paul panicked and quickly threw home to get Dellucci, but the throw was off target, allowing Dellucci to score.

Carroll and Sizemore, meanwhile, weren't hanging around to watch the action. As the throw to the plate was on its way, they both decided to take the next bases themselves! All three were given credit for stolen bases, as both Carroll and Sizemore were in motion at the time of the mad dash for home by Dellucci.

I would loved to have been in the White Sox dugout for this one! Manager Ozzie Guillen was probably swearing up a storm in both English and Spanish! I gotta tell you, being anywhere close to Ozzie when he's going off is a lot of fun. You learn so much about his passion for the game and his philosophy about the game, and sometimes you even learn some new curse words or more creative ways to use them. Everybody should have the chance to be around for one of Ozzie's tirades, just once.

As far as Indians skipper Eric Wedge was concerned, he got to sit back and enjoy a play that no manager would ever draw up and was just happy to reap the rewards. I'm pretty sure they don't practice that play during spring training when they're working on their base running, but I can guarantee you one thing: Ozzie Guillen will have his team working on the elimination of that pickoff play as soon as he gets the chance.

In or Out?

If you had to pick a big-league stadium to visit on the Fourth of July, which would it be? If they don't have a hometown team to root for, I bet a lot of people would choose Yankee Stadium, especially if the Red Sox are in town. That's a place where you might see some real fireworks.

Thanks to a stubborn little ball that refused to pick a side, July 4, 2008, became a day that definitely belongs in this book.

The Red Sox had two on in the third inning with Kevin Youkilis at the dish. He hit a drive to deep left field that looked like it had a chance to be a three-run homer. Johnny Damon raced back to see if he could make the play.

Damon and the ball hit the left-field fence at the same time. It looked like Damon had just made a phenomenal catch, but as he crashed into the wall, the ball actually jarred loose from his glove and landed on *top* of the fence. It just sat there, halfway between being a home run and dropping back into the field of play. At this

Johnny Damon watches a ball defy gravity as it sits atop the Yankee Stadium fence in 2008.

point, the fans had realized what had happened, but a few heart-stopping seconds went by before Damon did. Directly behind Damon, one fan was going crazy, gesturing like mad to get Damon to turn around. By the time he did, the ball just casually rolled off the fence and back in play—no home run!

Injured and in serious pain after his collision with the wall, Damon scrambled over to the ball and heaved it back into the infield, holding Youkilis to a triple. After the play, Damon left the game clutching his injured shoulder.

Damon signed with the Yankees in 2006 after four years with the Red Sox.

As far as the umpires were concerned, the play wasn't called dead while Damon was reeling on the ground because the ball was still live, untouched, and in play. The play was scored as a hit, and Brett Gardner replaced Damon in left field. For the first time in his long 14-year career, Johnny was put on the disabled list.

I've never seen anything like that happen during a Yankees–Red Sox game. Maybe this particular ball was a Yankees fan.

Yankee Stadium's Roof Collapses

I've heard of canceling games for rain, lightning storms, tornadoes, but never because a roof was collapsing. That is, until it happened in New York in 1998.

Still smarting from their loss in the 1997 playoffs against the Indians, the Yankees wanted to get off to a smooth start in 1998, but the baseball gods had other ideas.

The date was April 13, 1998.

Right before batting practice, a large 500-pound section of the Yankee Stadium roof collapsed and crashed into the upper-deck seats. Luckily it happened right as batting practice was about to get underway, and not while the fans were in the stands, or someone would have been killed.

The game that night against the Angels was canceled, and one home game was played at Shea Stadium instead until the Yankee Stadium roof was repaired and deemed safe for the public. It was the first time that the Yankees had used Shea as their home since Yankee Stadium was renovated in 1974 and 1975.

It's fortunate for the Yankees that the section collapse didn't harm anybody, but most importantly the Yankees proved that they didn't even have to play on their own home field that year to win the World Series. They could do it while playing at Shea!

Matt Holliday Slides to the Playoffs

It was a perfect day for a Holliday.

All the Colorado Rockies needed to do was to win one game and they would win the wild-card and make it to the 2007 postseason. One ballgame! Heck, they had just won 13 of their last 14 games, so things were certainly going pretty well. The only guy to beat them during that streak was Brandon Webb of the Diamondbacks, the reigning Cy Young Award winner.

Baseball in Colorado never really had that much atmosphere, which is ironic considering the city itself is a mile high. Denver was always a football town. But this Rockies team was full of fighters. They had a great mix of scrappers, young talent, and veteran leadership. And they were on fire. They were in the middle of the best winning streak in their franchise's history. But when does the other shoe fall? When does the law of averages catch up with you?

Clint Hurdle had been patient with his team and had said all the right things while his boys were on their run, and in turn the fans started believing in their Rockies. Suddenly the mighty mountains weren't just a backdrop to the ballpark; they symbolized the strength of the entire team. And to know that they had played a full season, 162 games, just to get to this point and *still* needed another win against the Padres just to get in…that's pressure.

Matt Holliday was the team's young stud and he had the weight of the Rockies' playoff hopes on his shoulders. He had absolutely crushed the ball that season, but like the rest of the Rockies, he had to prove himself worthy of postseason play. Other players including Brad Hawpe, Garrett Atkins, and Rookie of the Year candidate Troy Tulowitzki were making a name for themselves on the national scene. And the heart of the franchise, Todd Helton, had hit a huge game-winning home run early in the streak against the Dodgers that made everybody on that team believe they had something special going on. Plus, believe it or not, the Rockies' *pitching* was amazing! Yeah, their pitching! This in a stadium where the balls have to be stored in a humidor just to keep a little moisture in them so that every fly ball doesn't end up being a home run. Jeff Francis was joined in the starting rotation by two kids nobody had ever heard of before, Ubaldo Jimenez and Franklin Morales, and their bullpen went 10–0 with a 2.07 ERA during the streak. It just seemed like it was meant to be.

But the Padres had plans of their own. They had not played well during the last week of the season, blowing opportunities that could

Matt Holliday slides across home plate—or did he? Either way, he put the Rockies into the playoffs in 2007.

have avoided this playoff game, but that didn't matter now. They had ace Jake Peavy on the mound, a guy who had won 19 games that year, would win the Cy Young Award, and was one of the toughest competitors in the game. And they had the all-time saves leader, Trevor Hoffman, waiting in the pen to close out any potential win.

Both teams had their chances to win this one and, as in any 13-inning game, both teams could point to a few plays that would have changed the eventual outcome. But this game came down to Matt Holliday standing on third base in a tie game with little Jamey Carroll at the plate. A base hit would win it, but why make it that easy?

Carroll lofted a fairly shallow fly ball out into right field and Holliday tagged up at third, ready to sprint for home with the winning run. Everything about the play was perfect: the run home by Holliday, the throw from the outfield, and the tag by Padres catcher Michael Barrett. Holliday literally took a nosedive into the plate, which I wouldn't recommend—but then again, I've never been trying to get somewhere that meant so much that fast before in my life. Have you?

It took a breathless second for all of us to learn the fate of the Rockies. After a slight hesitation, home-plate umpire Tim McClelland signaled "Safe!"

"Rocktober" was born that night. Colorado was jumpin' and there was a new "America's Team" for baseball fans to root for. Matt Holliday was now a national name with a scraped-up face and the Rockies were storming into the playoffs. After replays showed Holliday may have never actually touched the plate, Padres manager Bud Black downplayed the controversy by saying, "It looked like he touched it to me." Classy move on his part.

"I had no idea whether he was safe or not," teammate Tom Martin recalls. "All I cared about was that my teammates were in the playoffs. For me, there could be no more dramatic or crazy moment than sliding home to get to the playoffs."

What a run it was. The Rockies had won 14 out of their last 15 games. In 2002, Oakland had won 20 in a row and 23 of 24 in August and September, but not like this.

The Rockies blew away the Phillies in the Divisional Series and did the same to a stunned Arizona Diamondbacks team, winning seven straight playoff games to make it 21 out of 22. I think a lot of people were hoping the old saying about all good things coming to an end wouldn't be true this time. Unfortunately for them, Boston was waiting in the World Series.

Paul O'Neill is Quick on His Feet

Nicknamed "Ordeal" by the great Lee May, Paul O'Neill was a serious baseball player, to say the least. This guy practiced his batting stance even when he was standing in the outfield playing right field!

I think everybody remembers Paul as the fiery heart and soul of those Yankee championship teams of the late 1990s. They won the whole thing four times while he was there, so somebody should take note! He was so loved by Yankee fans, they chanted "Paul O'Neill! Paul O'Neill!" during the 2001 World Series while the Yankees were down in the final game at Yankee Stadium. The right-field faithful, as well as the rest of the capacity crowd of 57,000, rose to their feet and showered their favorite son with this chant over and over again until he acknowledged them by tipping his cap while running in from right field before the ninth inning.

I've never seen anything like that in my life!

But he also won a World Series title with Cincinnati in 1990 and actually grew up a Reds fan because he was from Columbus, Ohio. So while I could tell you about some of the crazy stuff he did in New York—like yelling at himself in the dugout or knocking down Gatorade coolers—I want to go back to his days with the Reds, when that temper and enthusiasm weren't quite as well known.

In 1989, the Reds were playing at the old Veterans Stadium in Philadelphia (what a dump that place was). Steve Jeltz was on second base representing the winning run for the Phillies. There was a base hit to right field and O'Neill came charging in to make the throw to the plate. In his desperation to make the play, he bobbled the ball....

Now this is where the facts get a little blurry. Most accounts say that faced with no other options, O'Neill reached out and purposely *kicked* the ball toward the infield!

My version of the story is different. When O'Neill bobbled that ball, he knew he was in trouble. Outfielders know they only get one shot—charge the ball, scoop it up cleanly, and let go of your best rocket shot to the plate—and maybe you'll have a play! If you happen to bobble it, drop it, follow it around to see what it eats…you've got no chance.

Paul O'Neill is now a color commentator for the Yankees.

O'Neill knew after losing his grip on that ball that Jeltz was streaking around third and on his way to giving the Phillies the win. He got frustrated, so he just kicked the ball as hard as he could. How did he know that he would kick it right to the cutoff man to keep Jeltz at third? How did he know that his reputation of having a great arm would force the third-base coach to hold Jeltz on the play? How did he know that that play would end up being one of the craziest plays of his career? I guess he wanted to be in the book. The look on O'Neill's face was priceless. He knew he got away with one that day.

One of the most commonly used slangs in baseball for making an error is, "He kicked it." After this play, I don't think they ever said that to Paul O'Neill.

CHAPTER SIX

It's All About the Fans

Steve Bartman

Where is Steve Bartman? Somebody must know.

I was in the broadcast booth for Fox during the Steve Bartman game in the 2003 NLCS. What a series: Florida came back from a 3–1 deficit to beat the Cubs and then went on to whip the Yankees for the World Series title. Was it Steve Bartman's fault? Well, if you think that, then place yourself in the same category as anyone who blames everybody but themselves for their own shortcomings, people who think their team can actually get beat by the umpires or officials, and people who need to get a life.

All Steve Bartman was doing was being a baseball fan, a Cubs fan. He paid a lot of money to buy a playoff ticket to see his favorite team win the game that would put them in the World Series for the first time in about 100 years. He even brought his glove. Never know—you might catch a foul ball.

Please come out of hiding, Steve—it wasn't your fault.

The Cubs were just a few outs away from the biggest win in franchise history, and then the Marlins' Luis Castillo hit a lazy fly ball down the left-field line. Moises Alou got himself over to the wall and was in perfect position to make a difficult catch right in front of the first row of seats. And then…Steve Bartman tried to make the play instead! Alou was stunned…and pissed. Cubs fans were outraged and horrified—many of them commenting later that a "true Cubs fan" would have backed away from the ball so that Alou would have a clear path to make the play. That's BS: Bartman did exactly what any fan would do when a ball is coming right at him—he tried to catch it.

Alou himself said he didn't think he would've caught the ball even if Bartman hadn't interfered—of course, it took him five years

Attention Chicago Cubs: please win a World Series and get Steve Bartman off the hook.

to say it. I was there. I saw a hundred replays. I saw the position of everybody involved. Alou would have caught it. But there were no fewer than seven other people near Bartman who were trying to catch it, too. Those people should thank their lucky stars that they didn't get a piece of that ball, because if they did, they would be the ones in hiding, not Bartman, and they would have received the death threats and watched the helicopters flying over their houses. They would have had their names and addresses printed in the paper so that every Cubs fan—hell, every baseball fan—would know exactly who they could blame for the Cubs' failure. Their lives would have been turned into a living hell just like Bartman's was.

Come on out, Steve—it wasn't your fault.

The Cubs were up 3–1 in a seven-game series with Carlos Zambrano, Mark Prior, and Kerry Wood as the next three scheduled starting pitchers. But the Marlins were simply the team of destiny that season…not the Cubs.

Nobody's heard from Bartman since. Florida's chamber of commerce invited him to move down south. The Bartman costume was a big hit that Halloween. All because he loved the Cubs?

Shame on us.

Chad Kreuter Loses His Hat

California has this laid-back reputation, supposedly filled with good-looking blondes, beach bums, and surfer dudes.

Chad Kreuter is one of those California natives, having been born in Greenbrae, California.

But even the mellowest guys have their limits.

Kreuter had been around the game a long time. He had debuted with the Texas Rangers, and before it was all said and done, he had played for seven teams, the Los Angeles Dodgers being the seventh.

I don't think Kreuter could have ever imagined when he was sitting in the bullpen on May 16, 2000, at Wrigley Field, that his *cap* would have an itinerary all of its own.

Now, Chicago is definitely a city that encourages mixing it up once in a while. I should know, as I played for the White Sox on the south side of town. But Wrigley Field is on the north side. Cubs fans are supposed to be the peacekeepers, the die-hard fans who just love the game, and if the Cubs win that's even better…right?

Chad played for seven teams over 16 big-league seasons.

Well, not always. More fans got ejected during this game than at any other game in the history of Wrigley Field—and all because of a hat! It didn't even have anything to do with the two teams playing the game or a bad call from an umpire. In fact, it was one of the few brawls I've ever seen where both teams were on the same side! It was the players vs. the fans! Yikes!

Apparently, the souvenirs they sell at Wrigley Field concession stands are not the type that fans really want. I guess they don't really have a legitimate use for that foam finger, don't really want the fake batting helmet that the ice cream comes in, and could care less about those leftover Matt Clement beards. What they really want—or at least what one guy wanted—was an authentic Dodgers cap. Game-worn, that day, by Chad Kreuter.

Sounds like a cool souvenir. But someone forgot to inform that dude that there is a word for that kind of behavior—assault.

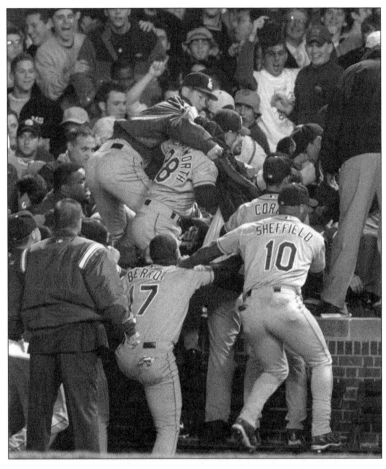

Chad Kreuter and the Dodgers follow his hat into the stands at Wrigley Field.

Wrigley Field has an issue with its bullpens. Always has. They're just too close to the stands and that can cause problems. The stadium is just so old that there's nowhere else to put them.

So Kreuter was out in the pen, minding his own business, when some idiot punches him in the back and steals the hat right off his head!

After the initial shock wore off, Chad turned around and went after his cap—and the guy! I don't know, maybe it was his lucky hat and he didn't want to lose it. Or maybe he just thought that it was wrong for somebody to think that they could do something like that. He wasn't alone. It only took a few seconds for the other players to notice what was happening, and Kreuter immediately had lots of help. Players from both teams were over to the Dodgers' bullpen, some of them following Chad into the stands. Fans were involved, pushing and shoving and trying to figure out why Kreuter was going nuts.

By the time it was all sorted out, both benches had emptied and the entire Dodgers team seemed to be in the right-field seats rather than on the field of play. And I thought Wrigley Field was supposed to be the friendly confines!

In the end, Kreuter did get the hat back, but it was a crazy ordeal that should have never happened. I know for a fact that Mitch Poole, the equipment manager for the Dodgers, would have given Chad a brand-new cap in about 10 seconds. As for the joker who tried to snag the hat right off Kreuter's head? I think $24 will probably get you the authentic New Era cap that all the big-leaguers wear, but he doesn't deserve one, at any price.

The Apple Doesn't Fall Far from the Tree

After being around professional baseball for 30 years, one of the reasons I keep going to the ballpark is that I think there's always something that can happen in a game that can make me say, "I've never seen anything like that before!"

But sometimes those moments can also be downright sad.

I've seen drunk guys antagonize players. I've seen fans run out on the field—heck, one lady even jumped into the on-deck circle with me at Yankee Stadium. She said somebody would pay her $250 to come onto the field and kiss me. I let her do it—I felt bad for her, since it was going to cost her at least $250 to get out of jail.

There have been brawls between players, brawls between players and fans, and brawls in the stands that have halted play because they got out of hand.

But I'd never seen a father and son attack a first-base coach before.

Then it happened in Chicago, during a game between the Kansas City Royals and the White Sox.

With today's security precautions, fans rarely get on the field, close to the field, or anywhere near their favorite players to get autographs, and by now you know I think that's a bad thing. Most players like to give autographs, but they can't. Security is literally everywhere.

Normally a fan can't make a move toward the field without police and security converging on him in a millisecond.

Yet, in September 2002, one year after 9/11, two fans—a father and son no less—ran onto the field in Chicago and attacked Royals first-base coach Tom Gamboa.

I couldn't believe my eyes when I saw the replays. It was brutal.

These two idiots, fueled by alcohol and drugs, decided it was a good idea to jump on the field to attack an innocent first-base coach. Hello? Reasoning?

They got to a surprised and horrified Gamboa in an instant, wrestled him to the ground, and started pummeling him with punches. Fortunately, the Royals saw what was happening and responded even faster than security could. Literally a dozen Royals descended on Gamboa's attackers. They not only protected their coach from the beating that he was taking but also took their liberties with the complete morons that were behind the ambush.

Security got on the field and separated the crazed father and son from Gamboa and half of the Royals team. I wish the Royals had about five minutes alone with the two guys.

It wasn't until arrest reports were filed that everyone found out the two morons were a father-and-son team; William Ligue Jr., 34, and his misguided son, 15, were the crazed duo who had the bright idea of jumping onto the field at Comiskey Park and causing trouble.

Aaron Rowand, then the center fielder for the White Sox, told the media immediately following the game that he thought he saw

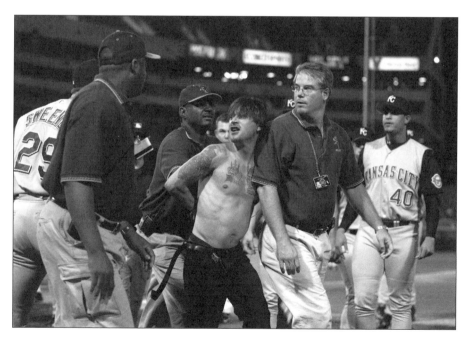

Security escorts knucklehead William Ligue Jr. off the field after he and his son attacked Royals coach Tom Gamboa in Chicago.

something fall out of the pocket of one of attackers. Rowand was not seeing things; it turned out that something was a pocketknife!

This wasn't just a Psycho moment; it could have really been a tragedy.

Everyone asked me what I thought about it and how, as a former player, it can be prevented in the future. I didn't have an answer.

How can anybody explain an incident as idiotic and ridiculous as this one? It's not security's fault. How can you anticipate every possible altercation that might happen at a ballgame with 40,000 people attending? The simple answer is that you can't. And I believe that most ballparks are very safe and the security staffs do an amazing job of keeping order. Some things you can't ever predict.

> Ligue and his son got 30 months of probation but didn't spend any time in jail.

Disco Demolition Night

Everybody remembers disco, don't they? I do! In fact I might be a little stuck in that era: of the six preset radio stations in my car, two of them play '70s dance music. Hey, I graduated from high school in 1978, cut me some slack.

Disco was the dance craze of the 1970s and early 1980s. There were shows on television like *Soul Train* and *Dance Fever*, and movies like *Fame* had kids dancing their heads off. *Saturday Night Fever* catapulted actor John Travolta into mega-stardom and the Bee Gees were kings of the dance floor.

Everyone seemed to like disco—except Chicago disc jockey Steve Dahl and the White Sox. They decided that the best thing to do was to hold an anti-disco night at Comiskey Park on July 12, 1979.

Dahl had been fired by a radio station that went to an all-disco format, and when he got another job at a different station, he spent most of his time badmouthing the genre.

The idea behind the night was simple: bring an unwanted disco album to the game and get into the doubleheader vs. the Detroit Tigers for 98 cents. Then, between games, they'd blow up the records and get rid of the disco era once and for all.

I guess a lot of people really hated disco because more than 75,000 fans showed up! One problem: Comiskey Park didn't hold 75,000 fans.

After the first game, Dahl and his cronies made their way out to center field and gathered thousands of records up and put them into a few crates—then blew them up! The instant the explosion went off, thousands of crazed disco haters stormed the field. Fires were started in the outfield and in the upper deck; a huge hole was blown in the outfield turf and riots were breaking out all over the field. The fans soon discovered that LPs doubled very nicely as Frisbees, and suddenly there were hundreds of flying projectiles everywhere. The batting cage was torn down and wrecked. It got so bad that the Chicago riot police had to be called in to restore order.

There were a lot of arrests, but just a few minor injuries. When things finally calmed down a little, Tigers manager Sparky Anderson said there was no way he would risk the safety of his players by letting them go out for the second game of the doubleheader. The White Sox had to forfeit the second game. To this day, it stands as the last American League game to be forfeited.

Obviously, what seemed like a good idea at the time turned out to be the most disastrous promotion of all time. Although the great innovator Bill Veeck caught a lot of the heat for what happened, many say it was his son Mike's big idea.

Seems like a lot of hate going around just because you don't like "Stayin' Alive."

Fans in Chicago take their hatred of disco to the extreme on Disco Demolition Night in 1979.

Morganna the Kissing Bandit

PSYCHO-METER

7.2

Known as the buxom and beautiful "Kissing Bandit," Morganna Roberts' measurements were officially recorded at 60–23–39.

She had been interviewed on *Late Night with David Letterman* and was on *The Tonight Show* with the legendary Johnny Carson. Her act was always the same, but like any great act, it never got old. Hey, why change a good thing?

She always had a front seat and wore a big jacket of some sort. Then she'd disrobe and run onto the field and plant a big kiss on a player of her choosing. She appeared in *Playboy* and the movie *Kingpin* and then retired to family life in the early part of this decade.

Her first kiss was on a dare from a friend; the recipient was none other than the great Pete Rose. I guess if you're going to launch a career of any sort, why not start with a Hall of Famer? Her other conquests included Frank Howard, George Brett, Cal Ripken Jr., Johnny Bench, Steve Garvey, Don Mattingly, Dickie Thon, Nolan Ryan, Steve Yeager, Len Barker, and Duane Ward. Morganna also dabbled in basketball and kissed a few NBA players, including Charles Barkley.

There will never be another Morganna, partly because today's ballparks have more security preventing fans from entering the field of play. She was one of a kind who remains a symbol of the age of free love—and of an era when players had to keep their heads on a swivel in case somebody was jumping out of the stands ready to plant a big kiss on them!

Jeffrey Maier Calls Off Tony Tarasco

Game 1 of the 1996 ALCS between Baltimore and New York was the Yankees' first appearance in the championship round in quite some time. They had lost to Seattle in the ALDS the year before, where they had to watch nutty Mariners fans scoop up dirt at home plate in the Kingdome in celebration of defeating the hated Yankees. Before that, they hadn't been to the postseason since 1981 when they lost to the Dodgers in the World Series.

Jeffrey Maier, a 12-year-old kid from New Jersey, was about to make sure their return was a triumphant one.

Trailing Baltimore 4–3 in the eighth inning, shortstop Derek Jeter, then a rookie, hit a towering fly ball off Orioles relief pitcher Armando Benitez. It should have been caught by Tony Tarasco, who had replaced Bobby Bonilla in right field. That's when the fireworks began.

Tarasco thought he was robbing Jeter of an extra-base hit; miraculously, that fly ball became a home run, all with a little help from a good-luck charm positioned out in right field.

As Tarasco went to make the catch, Maier, a lifelong Yankees fan who had received a ticket to the game as a bar mitzvah present, reached his glove over the wall and deflected the ball into the stands, sending the Orioles into a fury. Jon Miller, the Orioles' radio announcer at the time, called it "fan interference," as did the Orioles themselves. But the umpires huddled together and ruled no fan interference—home run for Jeter! Maier was escorted out of the stadium. If it wasn't fan interference, why escort him out of the park? That usually only happens to overzealous ball hawks or drunk

Jeffrey Maier pulls a reverse Bartman and helps the Yankees beat the Orioles in the 1996 ALCS.

guys running onto the field. If the umpires had ruled that Maier did interfere, then the home run would have been called back and Jeter would've been called out.

The Yankees won that game 5–4 and went on to win the series in five games. Maybe they should have voted Maier a share of the playoff money since he did launch them into the World Series.

That was a pivotal game, statistically and emotionally for the Yankees, and Baltimore never recovered. Hey, maybe George Steinbrenner should have drafted Maier to help out in the outfield! The Orioles have talked to Maier about playing for them now that he is out of college—he certainly showed he had good instincts.

Maier is the all-time hits leader at Wesleyan University in Connecticut.

Funny, but anything can happen in a short postseason series, and once you get into the head of a team, you stay there until the series is over. Whether everyone wants to admit it or not, psychology does play a role in sports, and once a guy or team or stadium is inside a player's head, there's a problem. That play by Maier definitely swung the pendulum to the Yankees' favor big time.

Ten years later, during his senior year at Wesleyan, Maier still heard it from Baltimore fans as they threw ice and snow at him, looking for revenge for what they thought was him stealing victory from the Orioles. He even appeared in a documentary made by an Orioles fan called *I Hate Jeffrey Maier*. Even Jeter recently said that he could never forget what Maier did for him and for the Yankees organization, and Maier still claims Jeter is his favorite Yankee.

That will probably go down as the best bar mitzvah present in New York Yankees history.

The Red-Haired Wacko

As a former major leaguer, I can tell you that players seldom notice the wacky stuff going on around them because they are concentrating on the game. There's an old adage that fireworks could be set off without a player knowing it, and that's probably true. There is a delicate balance within any athlete; you're taught to be aware of everything while at the same time blocking out certain things so as to not lose focus on what's most important.

But sometimes, like when a red-haired streaker hits the field in subzero temperatures, it's hard not to notice!

Unfortunately, even the most desperate of housewives didn't really want to see what they witnessed at Coors Field when the Brew Crew was in town.

Games at Coors Field in Colorado can get rather brutal because of the elements, so the first thing that usually comes to mind is finding a concession stand that sells hot chocolate. The last thing on most people's minds is taking off their clothes and running laps on the field. But for one special fan, that idea seemed like a great one, so he dropped his drawers and did just that. It made an impression on the crowd and on one David Weathers, then a relief pitcher for the visiting Brewers.

"I'll never forget it as long as I live," he said. "Okay, so here I was warming up in the bullpen. We were fighting for contention, so I was pumped to get into the game. I'm concentrating on my throws and loosening up. All of a sudden, this guy with flaming red hair appears. I don't just mean reddish hair, I mean flaming red hair. He's also got this crazed look about him, but I didn't pay him any further attention, other than the fact that his red hair caught my eye because he was right behind the top of the bullpen where I looked after my warm-ups. I resumed warming up and the crowd behind the bullpen suddenly erupted. The moment I turned my head to see what was going on, I saw the same dude totally naked! He wasn't even well endowed! Imagine being nude and not well hung! He ran onto the field. The crowd went wild. The cops came. They chased him around the right-field area. He ran away. They chased him toward center. He ran away. They finally got him down and carried him away in handcuffs. The fans were hysterical."

Streaking was a bad idea back in the '70s and it's still a bad idea today, especially on cold days when "shrinkage" might be involved. The bottom line is, keep it to yourself. Don't try it at Coors Field or any other major sporting event—you may end up naked and sitting on the cold, hard floor of the county jail.

The Curse of David Ortiz?

Almost all of the crazy things that we talk about in this book happened on the field or at least around a field, but once in a while something happens before a field is even *built*.

The Yankees didn't expect to start an excavation project on the site of their brand-new stadium before it even opened; heck, they hadn't even started tearing down the old place. But that's what they wound up doing, and the reason sent shivers down the spine of every Yankee fan—some Red Sox fan had buried a David Ortiz jersey in the foundation of the stadium!

Workers pull a David Ortiz jersey out of the new Yankee Stadium's foundation, foiling Red Sox fan Gino Castignoli's fiendish plan to curse the hated Yankees.

The jersey had been buried by Gino Castignoli, one of the construction workers on the project who, even though he grew up in New York, was a Red Sox fan. A couple of the other construction workers found out about it and got scared; I guess they thought the fate of the Yankees' future now rested on their shoulders, so they ratted on poor Gino. At first, the Yankees were so mad they thought about pressing charges against the culprit. But come on, sending someone to jail for burying a Red Sox jersey? We all know there are much worse things buried in the foundations of buildings around this country.

The Yankees ended up donating the jersey to a Boston-based charity.

The Yankees decided that the shirt must be located and ripped out of the foundation immediately. It took five hours to figure out exactly where it was and another two to get it jackhammered out. Some people put a lot of faith in crazy stuff like that. The Curse of the Bambino, the Billy Goat curse in Chicago…I guess the Yankees wanted to avoid the Curse of the Buried Ortiz Jersey?

Cheap Beer Leads to Big Trouble

On June 4, 1974, at Municipal Stadium in Cleveland, the Indians held a promotion designed to increase sales of Stroh's beer. They sold each beer for 10¢.

You can smell something bad coming already, huh?

From a technical point of view, the team was right—sales of beer that night went through the roof. The only problem was when you sell beer for a dime, fans have a hard time drinking responsibly!

Sometimes drinking makes people sleepy; on this night, it made them loud, vulgar, anxious to fight, and willing to take their clothes off. The crowd became so unruly that riots broke out all over the stadium. Fans were ripping seats out with their hands—no socket wrenches needed. There was even a huge fire in the upper deck!

In the end, the game had to be forfeited by the Indians to the visiting Texas Rangers. And today, the 16-ounce beer at Dodger Stadium costs $12.

Rick Monday Saves Old Glory

So how often do you see fans run onto the field, hover over what looks like a campfire in center field, and then try to burn the American flag?

Today those idiots would be tackled by security about three seconds after they hopped the fence. After 9/11, nobody wants to have people running around on the field at a baseball game. But back in 1976, a couple of antiwar demonstrators actually ran onto the field and prepared to burn a flag at Dodger Stadium while the team was playing the Cubs.

What the two protesters didn't figure on was that the Cubs' center fielder, Rick Monday, had been in the Marine Corps Reserves and was nimble on his feet. So when Monday realized that these crazy fans were up to something, and when their intentions became clear, he just reacted. Swooping in just before the flag could be lit, Monday snatched it away and started running across the outfield with it!

Rick Monday, American hero, swipes Old Glory away from protestors in 1976.

Monday had his best season that year with career highs in home runs, runs scored, and RBIs. Coincidentally, he was traded the following season to the Dodgers, where he could patrol and protect center field full time.

The coolest part about the whole incident was the fans' reaction to Rick's heroics. They cheered and began to sing "God Bless America."

More than 30 years have passed since that day, but I'm proud to be a part of the annual celebration of that moment at Dodger Stadium. And it seems like there's even more attention paid to the event today than there was then, as if it somehow has more meaning to us given the current state of our world. Rick and his wife,

Barbaralee, travel all over the country accepting awards and speaking about what happened that day and what it means to him now.

Rick was the first person ever selected in the MLB draft.

I think the Dodger Stadium scoreboard summed it up nicely when Monday came up to the plate for his next at-bat that day. It read, "Rick Monday...You made a great play."

A Fan Makes a Pitching Change

Baseball is getting almost as bad as football when it come to

technological changes. Wait, I take that back—nothing will ever be as bad as football, where every team has 12 coaches with headsets, plus cameras all over the place and microphones in the players' helmets. The quarterback gets high-resolution pictures of the opposing defense between series. He's constantly on the phone or has a headset wrapped around his head talkin' to somebody. The coaches have cell phones, earphones, and headphones at their disposal the entire game, along with a pair of binoculars. Today's players are no doubt tremendously talented, but do we ever see them just react and play football, or are they just programmed robots who do exactly what they're told to do? I'd love to find out. Take the coaches out of the rafters of the stadium, leave the headphones and the rest of the electronics at Best Buy, teach the playbook to your team, teach your quarterback how to read a defense, and just go play football.

But back to baseball. Today's players have videos of almost every swing a hitter has ever taken and every pitch an opposing pitcher has ever thrown. There are advanced scouting reports on every player, even guys down in the minor leagues. The information now available to the players far exceeds the information available to me when I played, and you're a fool if you don't take advantage of it to make yourself a better player. It will never be as complicated as football, but I wonder how long it will be before I start to have some of those same feelings about baseball. Instant replay has already arrived, after all.

I guess I just love the fact that if the third-base coach wants to communicate with the hitter or the base runner, he has to use signs to do it so everybody in the ballpark doesn't know what he's talkin' about. Bunt, hit and run, steal—it's all in code. It's comical to watch the coach go through his signs like he's scratching a bad rash, all so he can hide his intentions from the other team. It's a simple system reminiscent of a simpler time. I suppose pretty soon every batting helmet will be fitted with a listening device hooked up to a microphone stuck to the coach's chest. Then all he has to do is whisper, "Bunt." That's no fun.

As a matter of fact, there was a time when communicating on the field was so low-tech, it seemed like anybody could get involved. The fans were so close to the action that they could have running conversations with some of the players and coaches during the game, and many did just that. The Brooklyn Dodgers had a fan like that in Hilda Chester. This woman was a leather-lunged lifer who attended every game and rooted her brains out for her Dodgers. One night, sensing the game was not going their way, she took matters into her own hands.

Dodgers manager Leo Durocher was watching his pitchers struggle when he was handed a slip of paper by outfielder Pete Reiser.

"Bring in Hugh Casey," the note read.

"So he walked out of the dugout, and made the change," recalls Carl Erskine.

The move didn't work—Casey was lit up!

Larry MacPhail was the team president at the time and Durocher was steaming mad. "You tell that MacPhail the next time he wants to make a change he can forget about it!" Erskine remembers an angry Durocher yelling at Reiser, the message-bearer.

"But Larry didn't give me that note," explained Reiser.

"He didn't?" a bewildered Durocher said. "Then who the heck did?"

"Hilda Chester," replied a sheepish Reiser.

If only Leo had a headset and some better communication equipment set up between himself and MacPhail….

CHAPTER SEVEN

That's *Gotta* Hurt!

It Ain't Easy Being an Italian Sausage

Sometimes singing "Take Me Out to the Ballgame" during the seventh-inning stretch just isn't enough for fans. They want more. They want the chicken dance, or the "kiss cam," or maybe even a marriage proposal. All due respect to big-league baseball, but the minor leagues have completely outdone the big-league teams in the innovation and fun departments. The crazy things they do between innings at minor-league games across the country are amazing. Races around the bases, giveaways, local promotions, you name it—those teams have to compete for people's entertainment dollars and they really make it fun for the whole family.

The Milwaukee Brewers have the "Sausage Race" at every home game. It's completely tired and outdated, but now it's as much a part of a Brewers game as the game itself. It's a totally harmless race between five different mascots dressed as meat products (they recently added the fifth—the chorizo—to the group). The Washington Nationals have recently added the "Presidents Race" to their entertainment lineup— Lord knows they need something—where Teddy, Abe, and a few other dead dignitaries race to the finish line. Here's a tip if you're betting on this race: Teddy, with his huge smile and monocle, never wins.

But back in 2003, there were just four people involved: a hot dog, an Italian sausage, an oversized bratwurst, and a Polish sausage. I know that over the years there were players who dressed up and took the challenge—I can't believe I never jumped into the Polish for a quick run myself!

Randall Simon whacks a mascot during the Sausage Race in Milwaukee; I guess he prefers chicken!

So on July 9, 2003, the seventh-inning stretch came and the race was on.

The crowd loved it. The players lined up and watched before they went back onto the field.

But then Randall Simon, who was playing for the Pirates at the time, got a little bored, I guess, so he decided to get in on the act. Not as one of the sausages, but as a sideshow.

As the Italian sausage ran by the Pirates' dugout, Randall took a swing at it with his bat!

I don't know what he was thinking—he wasn't thinking, most likely—but he obviously forgot that inside that costume was a 19-year-old college girl named Mandy Block. Poor Mandy fell to the ground after getting whacked in the head. Behind her was another young college girl named Veronica Piech. Veronica was inside the giant hot dog and also toppled over when Mandy hit the ground.

While Simon and Block laughed it off, the league office did not—Simon was suspended for three games.

Commissioner Bud Selig swiftly apologized for Simon's actions as fans called the radio stations in Milwaukee to whack Simon the way he whacked that sausage.

Twice a year, the sausages race against their Pittsburgh counterparts, the Racing Pierogies.

Simon was questioned by the sheriff's office, but no charges were filed and he got off with a $432 fine. It was a good thing nobody was seriously hurt or the story would have never gone away and Simon would have been explaining his actions for years to come.

Of course, he was happy to apologize many times over and even autographed the bat for Block. I guess you just have to list this one in the "I thought it was a good idea at the time" department.

Frankie Francisco Tosses a Chair

What do you do when some drunk guy is verbally abusing you while you're trying to play? Do you snap back at him? Do you kill him with kindness and hope he quiets down? Or do you just try to ignore him and act like he's not even there? How about standing up and throwing a chair at the guy?

Frankie Francisco had had enough, and he chose option No. 4. Try explaining that move to Bud Selig.

On September 13, 2004, Texas Rangers pitcher Frankie Francisco got fed up with the hecklers in Oakland. And when I say fed up, I mean fed up, fueled up, and chaired up!

Every major leaguer has his least-favorite park because of hecklers. Some pitchers hate Fenway because the bullpens are so close to the bleacher creatures. Some hate Yankee Stadium because… well, because you're a visiting player in Yankee Stadium. Frankie apparently hated Oakland Coliseum. The fans out there have never been mousy, but they also aren't known to be tough, either. But it was plainly obvious, even on television, that Francisco was being heckled and that it was pretty personal, judging by his reactions leading up to the big blowup.

Having had enough of this guy's foul and abusive mouth, Frankie took a plastic chair from the bullpen area alongside the stands and fired it right into the crowd. I don't know what it says about his pitching ability, but he missed the guy—from point-blank range.

Unfortunately, however, he did clock the guy's wife! (Insert your own bad joke about how it's always the woman's fault—I'm staying out of it.)

So now you have this bloodied woman, peeking out from under a bullpen chair that just got hurled onto her. She's pissed at Francisco for throwing it, and at her husband for causing it all.

You can just smell the lawsuit, can't ya?

So could Major League Baseball and the Texas Rangers. Owner Tom Hicks wasn't too happy about all the publicity his club was receiving on the national front. Rule of thumb—it's always good for an owner to hoist a World Series banner in center field before settling a huge lawsuit.

Major League Baseball suspended Francisco and there was talk about prosecution outside the ballpark. The bottom line is that fans know that their ticket entitles them to free speech, and a lot of what comes out of their mouths isn't fit to print. Seriously, I learned a whole lot of stuff about my mother that I never knew when I played for the Red Sox and visited Yankee Stadium for the first time.

Most fans are at the game to cheer on their team and have a good time, but some are there after a bad day, had one cocktail too many, or are just downright mean. They are the ones who may cause trouble or take their frustrations out on the players—but that's better than them going home and kicking their dogs. Players have always been expected to perform above a normal person's tolerance level and assume that it's not always going to be a pleasant experience at the ballpark. But don't think that paying for your ticket means you can do anything you want to the players. I listened to people tell me that I sucked, and tried to ignore the childish gestures. Heck, I even forgave the bad language. But if anybody had ever touched me or threw something at me or tried to harm me in any way, I'd have gone all Ron Artest on 'em. I totally disagree with all those experts that say a player never has the right to take a swing at a fan. It shouldn't happen—but *never*? I believe that we all have the right to protect ourselves, so if you mess with me or my family, you've crossed the line and all bets are off.

That said, I can't recommend any young players ever following Frankie Francisco's lead when it comes to fan interaction!

Jason Kendall's Broken Ankle

It takes a lot to make me sick to my stomach. Heck, I've eaten "street meat" at 3:00 in the morning in New York City and lived to tell about it. (With the onions and peppers, it's pretty good. And the rolls are so soft!)

Jason Kendall suffers one of the grislier injuries in major-league history in 1999.

The fans in Pittsburgh on July 4, 1999, weren't so lucky. In one of the freakiest plays I've ever seen, Pirates catcher Jason Kendall ran to first base on a hard ground ball and fractured his ankle while touching first base.

Kendall had the throw beaten, but his ankle just slipped on the bag a little and then snapped—in full view of the television cameras and all the fans. Plays like this have happened before: there was Robin Ventura sliding into home and having his ankle literally turned backward, and Moises Alou tearing his ligaments and breaking his ankle on a bad slide into second base while playing for the Expos. So why does Kendall's injury make this book?

First of all, there are a lot of injuries in baseball, and they're never pretty. The athlete, whether he's a superstar or the last guy on the bench, has to contemplate rehab or retirement—neither of which are options anybody wants to think about. Retirement means starting over and facing the big question—what do you do with the rest of your life? Imagine you're 28, you don't have a college degree, you've put all your eggs into the baseball basket, and you get injured. You have bills from four years ago when you were in Double A and were drowning in debt because you only made $1,400 a month for the six-month season; during the off-season, you're on your own. Your home is in Oregon but you're playing in Connecticut, and it's your responsibility to get your family back and forth, rent an apartment, find some furniture, set up the utilities, and still have enough left over to pay the rent on an empty house back home. Your kids barely recognize you because they're in school until June and you left for spring training in February. Everybody back in your hometown is counting on you, telling all their friends that they knew somebody who was going to make it big. And don't forget the missus—she put her whole life on hold for you, and a promising career in the nursing field will never happen now. You're sick of the BS and think this may be the time to just hang 'em up and find a real job. Doing what?

Kendall came back to make the All-Star team in 2000.

So yeah, if you're good enough to make it to the big leagues, you're gonna rehab that injury and not give up until it's absolutely necessary.

At that point in his career, Jason Kendall was the next *it* guy for the Pirates organization and for Major League Baseball. He was a young guy with a lot of talent, a great heart, a great personality, and tons of grit. But I guarantee you that the Pirates were looking for another catcher to replace him as soon as he went down.

Mark Loretta was playing first base that day for the Brewers, and right after that ball went into his glove he saw Jason hit the ground like he'd been shot down by a sniper.

"I actually saw the bone shoot straight through his pants," recalls Loretta, still physically squeamish after almost a decade. "The sound was sickening."

While Jason recovered from his injury, he's never been quite the same offensive threat. But his toughness is still plain to see, as he catches more games every year than almost every other guy in the league.

The baseball basket. You wouldn't put all your eggs in it, would you?

Rodney McCray Blasts through a Wall

One of the craziest plays I've ever seen has been replayed so often that if you haven't seen it, you're not a sports fan. And believe it or not, it didn't even happen in a major-league game. Playing for the Triple A Vancouver Canadians in the Pacific Coast League, Rodney McCray ran down a ball hit by Portland's Chip Hale on May 27, 1991.

However, someone forgot to inform McCray that you have to stop trying to catch the ball when you run out of stadium; McCray ran full speed right through the wall! He didn't just hit the wall—heck, we've seen that a million times. He actually *broke right through the right-field fence* and lived to tell about it. He got banged up a little, a few cuts and a lot of bruises, but adding insult to those injuries was the fact that he didn't even catch the ball!

What ever happened to communication with your center fielder? He's the one person in the house who should have been McCray's eyes and ears. It sounds like this: "You're all right, you're all right… track!…track!…*fence!*"

I actually played with Rodney and he was a pretty good outfielder. The White Sox called him up to the majors, but instead of using him as an outfielder, they used him more as a pinch runner! I guess they liked his ability to run through a play…or wall.

He has such a great attitude about the whole thing. He's a little like me in the sense that he knows that if that play had never happened, nobody would know who he was. "Man, I've got a bobblehead doll, my name is up on the wall in Portland—they renamed that part of the wall 'McCray's Alley,' so it's all cool," he said.

Rodney now works in the Dodgers' minor-league system as, you guessed it, an outfield coach.

Pete Rose Knocks Out Ray Fosse

Historically, the All-Star Game has always been filled with pomp and circumstance. Which team won or lost the game didn't really matter. The National League and American League flip-flopped home-field advantage in the World Series, so the game was just a little break in the middle of the season and a good excuse to have a party—oh yeah, and to honor the best players in the game. The home-run derby and fan fest are recent additions to the event. Back in the day, the All-Star players just sat around at their hotel and talked to fans and answered a few questions from reporters.

Now the winner of the Midseason Classic actually gets home-field advantage during the World Series. What genius came up with that idea? Maybe I shouldn't criticize because I don't have any better ideas, but in reality there might be only one or two players at the

All-Star Game who actually benefit if their team wins. The rest of the guys just want to have fun.

I am proud to say, however, that the MLB All-Star Game is much more like the "real" game of baseball than any other all-star event. The NBA's All-Star Game is a slam-dunk fest with absolutely no defense at all, the NFL's Pro Bowl is such an afterthought that it's held *after* the season is over, and the NHL's game? Please, why do they even use a goalie?

But because the All-Star Game is played in the middle of the regular season, an injury is a legitimate concern for players and their teams. The last thing anybody wants to do is get hurt in an All-Star Game and hurt his team's chances at making the playoffs. But most ballplayers only know how to play the game at one speed, and if you're in the game, your natural competitiveness usually takes over.

Put Pete Rose in that category. I don't think Rose ever did anything at less than 100 percent intensity at all times.

And in 1970, at the All-Star Game in Riverfront Stadium in Cincinnati, Pete proved that, exhibition game or not, he was there to compete. Remember, back then the entire league was different. Rivalries were stronger and the name on the front of your shirt meant more than the one on your back. Saying "hi" to your buddy on the other team was virtually unheard of; some guys actually hated players who played for other teams.

So in the bottom of the twelfth inning with the game on the line and Pete Rose on second base, what did anybody think Charlie Hustle was going to do if he had a chance to cross home plate? Sidestep Ray Fosse to avoid a collision? Pull up and let Fosse make the easy tag? Not a chance. Rose lowered his shoulder and steamrolled Fosse, sending him ass over tea-kettle, separating his

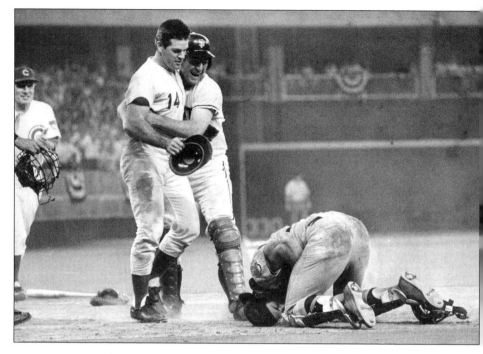

Pete Rose bowls over Ray Fosse during the 1970 All-Star Game in Cincinnati.

shoulder. Many people have criticized Rose for being too serious about a game that meant nothing. And many others have said that Ray Fosse was never the same player afterward. I don't know if that's true. Fosse had consecutive Gold Gloves in 1970 and 1971, but he never won another one after that. On the other hand, he also won two World Series rings, caught Dennis Eckersley's no-hitter, and played for eight more years in the big leagues.

Any way you look at it, this was a crazy play that still gets debated to this very day. If it's any consolation to Fosse, when Rose was sentenced to five months in prison for tax evasion, he was sentenced to a facility in Marion, Illinois—Fosse's hometown.

Albert Belle Bowls Over Fernando Vina

Albert Belle would never be selected as an instructor for anger management seminars.

He's more likely to be enrolled in one.

Upset about being hit with a pitch during a game against Milwaukee in 1996, he decided the best way to settle the matter was through an act of vengeance.

Albert, I guess, wanted to send a message to the opposition. His message was, *Hurt me and you'll be hurt.* But he picked on the wrong guy in Fernando Vina, the Brewers' second baseman. Vina always had a genial nature about him. A scrappy player, but not pugnacious, he was a good guy whom everybody liked. After his baseball days were over, he even became a commentator for ESPN.

Nevertheless, Vina was the victim of choice for Belle.

Two batters after Belle was hit, a slow roller was hit to Vina at second base—a possible double-play ball. Everybody knows the cardinal rule about never letting the second baseman tag you if you are the runner between first and second base. You have to make the fielder make a throw, either to first or second. So when Vina went to make the tag on Belle, Albert (don't call me Joey) didn't bother trying to avoid the tag—he just threw a vicious forearm shiver at Vina and stopped him for no gain.

Ordinarily, if you observed a play like that, you might be inclined to chalk it up to frustration after being hit by the pitch at the plate. But Belle had been known for so many other off-the-wall, unexplainable, stupid, and downright mean plays in his career,

Albert Belle shows no remorse after steamrolling Milwaukee's Fernando Vina in 1996.

that this was just another on the long list—no benefit of the doubt was headed his way. Surely you remember Belle blowing up at the media numerous times, threatening a photographer if he continued to take his picture, and throwing a fastball from point-blank range at the chest of a fan. Sometimes good players are bad guys—and they do crazy things.

One Halloween, Belle raced down some rowdy trick-or-treaters with his car.

Unbelievably, the umpires did not rule an automatic double play for the tackle Belle threw on Vina. For his trouble of being in the right place at the wrong time, Vina needed hospital attention at the end of the game. A tough price to pay for doing your job.

CHAPTER EIGHT

Once in a Lifetime

Dodgers Give Padres the Blues

Dodgers win 11–10! Sure, it sounds like a fun game to witness, but that doesn't even scratch the surface of the story of this night. On September 18, 2006, the Dodgers tied a major-league record as four hitters hit back-to-back-to-back-to-back home runs in a single inning. But this happened in the bottom of the ninth inning—to tie the game! To top it all off, it was against the hated Padres while both teams were fighting for first place in the NL West.

Just to set things up, I was headed out to my usual postgame-show perch behind the center-field wall, preparing to talk about another Dodgers loss. San Diego was up 9–5, and Padres closer Trevor Hoffman was warming in the pen, just in case. Over, right?

Not quite.

Jon Adkins was pitching and must have figured, *I'll just throw strikes, I've got a four-run lead.* So he pumped one in to Jeff Kent, who promptly launched a solo shot to left. No big deal, except that the next hitter, J.D. Drew, hit one into the right-field seats for back-to-back jacks. That made it 9–7, and the Padres weren't taking any more chances. They brought in the all-time saves leader to shut the door: enter Trevor Hoffman. Dodgers fans were starting to get into it and began to think something big might happen. Before they could take another breath, Russell Martin jumped the yard against Hoffy! At that point, I'm looking at my postgame partner, Kevin Kennedy, and we're both still a little pessimistic because, let's face it, between the two of us we think we've seen it all. But baseball is all about a bunch of kids dreaming about being part of a game like this. So we're laughing and joking and saying to each other, "No way."

Nomar Garciaparra explodes after his walk-off homer beats the Padres in 2006, the Dodgers' fifth home run in the game's final two innings.

Along came the most unlikely of candidates to keep the rally going. Part-timer Marlon Anderson stepped up to the plate and defied the odds. Anderson crushed another Hoffman offering into the seats and the place went nuts! Four straight bombs to tie it up in the ninth! We love to use the word *unbelievable* to describe things— it's such an overused cliché. But this was truly unbelievable!

The feeling was short-lived, however, because the Dodgers couldn't pull off the miracle of five straight homers and then gave up the lead run in the top of the tenth. After what everybody had witnessed in the ninth, I don't think anybody thought the Dodgers would have the energy or magic to do it again one inning later. It was destined to be one of those great comebacks that fell just short and was soon forgotten.

Nomar Garciaparra decided to be the guy who wouldn't let the dream die. With a runner on and the score 10–9 Padres, Nomar left us all in awe. You don't see much emotion out of Nomar; he plays hard, he plays well, he doesn't say much, and he goes home. Nobody had to watch the monstrous blast that was a "no doubter" as soon as he made contact. We just watched Nomar, fists thrust toward the sky in pure joy and triumph, leaping into the air as he made his way around the bases screaming at nobody and everybody all at the same time. The scene at home plate was World Series–worthy. 11–10 Dodgers. Crazy.

Nobody had ever seen Garciaparra so pumped up, so animated, so overcome with what he had seen in the ninth and what he had just pulled off in the tenth. But then again, nobody had *ever* seen what we saw that night.

Six Pitchers, One No-Hitter

Whenever the subject of no-hitters comes up, many different games come to mind. Hey, pick your favorite. There's Johnny Vander Meer's feat of back-to-back no-hitters, an accomplishment that will probably never be broken. Think about it: in order to break that record, you'd have to throw *three* straight no-hitters!

I also think of Nolan Ryan's many no-nos. He threw no-hitters for three different teams—the Angels, Astros, and Rangers. David Wells had his perfect game; whether he was sober or not, only Boomer really knows. David Cone tossed a perfect game of his own, and Doc Gooden threw a no-hitter—once both had left the Mets, ironically. And of course Harvey Haddix, who threw 12 innings of no-hit ball but doesn't get the credit he deserves.

However, the wackiest no-hitter of all time has to be the one thrown against the Yankees in 2003 by the Astros—because it was a *team* no-hitter, not an individual one! Huh? Yeah, the team got credit for a no-hitter.

On June 11, 2003, *six* pitchers for the Houston Astros combined on a no-hitter against the Yankees at Yankee Stadium. It definitely scores high on my Psycho-Meter because it didn't really feel like a no-hitter, even though it qualifies according to MLB rules. Roy Oswalt left the game after only one inning due to injury, and from the second inning on it was left to the bullpen to keep it going.

The Astros' hitters did their part. The offense scored eight runs and left the pitching end of things up to Pete Munro, Kirk Saarloos, Brad Lidge, Octavio Dotel, and Billy Wagner. In the ninth, Wagner struck out Jorge Posada and Bubba Trammell and then got Hideki Matsui to ground out to preserve this historic six-pitcher no-hitter.

Embarrassed as they might have been, the Yankees nevertheless did the classy thing. They sent bottles of champagne to each of the six pitchers and had them placed at their lockers by game's end. Heck,

None of the five Astros relief pitchers involved in this game are still with the club.

this one deserved to be celebrated—the last time the Yankees had been no-hit at Yankee Stadium was all the way back on August 25, 1952, by Detroit's Virgil Trucks.

To make matters worse for New York, the Yankees were in the middle of a hitting slump that had George Steinbrenner's blood boiling. Can't say that I blame the guy; after being no-hit by six different pitchers in your own park in an interleague game, it's pretty hard to find a silver lining. Lucky for George, only 29,905 attended the game!

Double Triple Plays

Every time I played third base, or any other position for that matter, I always tried to think of every possible play that might happen before the pitch was thrown.

My dad used to say, "Keep your head up and you'll never have to put it down." He also used to say 90 percent of the game is just standing around, so use that time to figure out what you're gonna do with the ball if it gets hit to you.

What am I going to do with runners on base if the ball is hit to my left, and how does that change if it's hit to my right? If it's a slow roller, can I still turn two or do I just get the out at first? What if there's a gapper—do I stay at third, or do I have to get to the cutoff position? What if the runners try to steal—how long can I hold my position before covering the bag, and what if the ball gets hit to me while they're stealing? Those are just a few of the things that are running through the minds of every player on the field before every pitch. If you pay close attention at a ballgame, you can sometimes see players talking to themselves while running through all the different scenarios. It really is one of the fun parts of the game that you rarely hear anybody talk about, mostly because it isn't something that the fans can see for themselves.

So any time there were runners on first and second with nobody out, I always thought about the same thing—I hoped the ball got hit just two steps to my right so I could grab the ball, touch third for one out, and then throw it on to second and then first for a triple play! But it never happened for me (or to me, for that matter).

Tom Brunansky knows the feeling—but from the hitter's perspective. When Bruno was with the Red Sox in 1990, he hit into a triple play against Minnesota that went just like the one I described—third to second and then on to first to get all three outs.

I suppose it would kinda suck being the hitter who starts a triple play. Your team is threatening, two guys on and nobody out—and you're up with a chance to drive the ball somewhere and score some runs. And then you hit the ball right to the third baseman and you know what's gonna happen even before you've taken two steps out of the box. But triple plays don't happen that often, so if you're one of the guys who actually hits into one, after you calm down a little, maybe you might think it's kind of cool to be a part of history. *Maybe.*

Of course, you know there's more to this story. No way does bouncing into a triple play make the book of the 100 most outrageous moments in baseball history.

The Twins actually lost this game 1-0!

So what if it happened twice in the same game? That might make it. And what if it happened exactly the same way twice—third to second to first in that game?

Brunansky hit into his triple play in the fourth. In the eighth, it was Jody Reed's turn to ground one down to Gary Gaetti, who stepped on third, tossed it to Al Newman at second, then watched the ball go on to Kent Hrbek at first for another triple play.

It was the first time in major-league history that any team had hit into two triple plays in the same game. Talk about a lousy day at the plate!

Fisk Wishes a Home Run at Fenway

The image of Carlton Fisk wishing that ball to stay fair at Fenway in the 1975 World Series is legendary. Nearly everybody in my parents' generation can tell you exactly where they were and what they were doing the moment they heard President Kennedy had been assassinated. For sports fans my age, the same can be said for Fisk's home run.

Like many great moments in sports history, we often remember the big moment, but rarely the events that led up to it. And if you somehow forgot what Game 6 in 1975 was all about, let me refresh your memory: it was one of the greatest World Series games ever played.

The weather leading up to that night had been terrible. There were three straight days of rain before Game 6, so the pitching rotations were rearranged and Boston was able to come back with Luis Tiant, who had already won Games 1 and 4 for the Red Sox. Tiant threw 163 pitches in the complete-game win in Game 4. A manager would get shot if he let a pitcher do that today, and, frankly, I don't know if there's a pitcher out there that would have the balls to try it.

The Big Red Machine countered with Gary Nolan. Fred Lynn hit a three-run shot in the first but also injured a rib trying to make a great catch on a Ken Griffey triple that scored two runs in the fifth inning. Big George Foster, whom I later played with in Chicago, hit a two-run double in the seventh inning and Cesar Geronimo went deep an inning later to make the score 6–3 Reds. Bernie Carbo, who already hit a pinch-hit home run in Game 3, hit a huge three-run shot to tie it for Boston in the eighth. And then the Red Sox had the bases loaded in the ninth inning with nobody out and didn't score—a fact most people forget.

In the eleventh, Dwight Evans, whom I also played with in Boston, made a great home-run-saving catch on a Joe Morgan drive and doubled Griffey off of first. That set the stage for Fisk in the bottom of the twelfth.

Facing Reds pitcher Pat Darcy, the eighth pitcher used by Reds manager Sparky Anderson, Fisk lofted a towering fly, as if scooping it into baseball heaven, toward the Green Monster in left. The only question was whether the ball was going to stay fair or go foul. It stayed fair and actually struck the foul pole for the 7–6 game winner.

Ironically, those images of Fisk hopping and jumping down the line should never have been shot; the cameraman who shot it was

One of the most iconic moments in baseball history: Fisk's home run in 1975.

supposed to follow the flight of the ball but was distracted (some say by a rat) and he kept his focus on Fisk instead.

The image of Fisk is an important part of baseball history partly because of what it represents—genuine eternal optimism. Today you see guys celebrate and dance or stand and watch home runs, but you never see a guy running sideways, motioning with his hands like a flagman at a construction site for the ball to stay fair. And we may never see it again.

I got the chance to play with Fisk in Chicago. For more than four seasons with the White Sox, I never saw a more deliberate, dedicated player than Fisk. He understood what it would take to be physically able to compete into his forties, and he was an excellent example of what a blue-collar work ethic and a load of talent can produce. He would stay after games, sometimes until 1:00 in the morning, lifting weights and getting extra work in before going home. He was a true leader in every sense of the word. These days, I see some players getting superstar money and they think the rules don't apply to them, that they can bend them to the point that the rest of the team starts to feel alienated and disrespected. All sports organizations should take a very close look at who the best player on their team is, because without the right guy, that team won't win.

The joy of that Game 6 home run was short-lived for Fisk and the Red Sox; the Reds took home the championship with a win in Game 7. Afterward, Fisk said, "We won three games to four." I guess sometimes when you're a winner like Carlton, you win even when you lose.

Fernando Tatis Slams Two in One Inning

At one point or another, we've all daydreamed about hitting a grand slam.

Any player who ever plays dreams of hitting a big home run someday, and if it's a really great dream, the bases are drunk when he does it. But I guess for Fernando Tatis, regular big-league dreams aren't good enough. In his baseball dream, he hits more than one grand slam. He hits two. And like they say, "If you dream big enough…."

On April 23, 1999, Fernando Tatis became the only player in major-league history to hit two grand slams *in one inning*! Don't pinch yourself, we're not dreaming this one up. And it gets better. He hit 'em both off the same pitcher.

Chan Ho Park was the unfortunate guy who served up both of those home runs to Tatis, allowing Fernando to set yet another record with eight runs batted in during one inning. This was during the Mark McGwire days of the Cardinals—Big Mac was the one hitting the home runs, not Fernando. Tatis hit 34 home runs that season, but he was no Mark McGwire. Chan Ho Park, likewise, was a battler and was not all that prone to serving up home runs. The odd combination made the event even more bizarre, as nobody would have ever predicted that Tatis would take Park deep, much less with the bases loaded, much less *twice* in the same inning with the bases loaded. What manager in his right mind would leave Park in the game long enough to give up two grannies? (It was Davey Johnson.) Ouch! The Cardinals really piled it on the Dodgers that night, but it's Tatis who received most of the credit.

Tatis laughs about it to this day, as he knows that no matter what he does for the rest of his career, he'll be known as the guy who hit two grand slams in the same inning off the same pitcher. Not bad.

Chan Ho doesn't laugh so much. When I asked him about it, he told me, "On the second one, he worked me to a full count, and with the bases loaded, the last thing I wanted to do was walk him." Well, maybe not the last thing….

Harvey Haddix Goes Perfect Through Twelve

There are tons of rules in baseball about what constitutes a no-hitter or a perfect game, but in the case of Harvey Haddix, those rules don't seem fair.

Let's look at some of the most memorable perfect games in baseball history. First off, you have Don

Larsen's perfect game in the 1956 World Series. Everyone who loves the history of baseball knows this one. The image of Yogi Berra jumping into Don's arms is something that every baseball fan has seen 100 times.

Then there was David Wells' perfect game in 1998, the year the Yankees ran away with the division, the league, and eventually the World Series. And for various reasons, Wells barely remembers it!

And then David Cone gave fans one to remember when he matched David Wells the following year with a perfect game in 1999. To make the game even more perfect, he accomplished this feat on the day Yogi and Larsen were in attendance to celebrate "Yogi Berra Day" at Yankee Stadium. George Steinbrenner made up with Yogi after a 14-year feud, and then Cone goes out and fires a gem of his own.

Those were all special, but one game was pitched every bit as well—maybe even better—yet no perfect game was credited.

On May 26, 1959, Harvey Haddix did the unthinkable: he took a perfect game into the *thirteenth inning*! Come on! Who does that in *any* era?

Imagine pitching 12 innings of no-hit, perfect ball. No walks, no hits, no errors—nothing! That's a full game and one-third of your next start in one night. Today that would never happen. Pitch counts, setup guys, left-handed specialists…don't get me started.

Haddix retired 36 consecutive batters, but he got no help from his offense.

Lew Burdette of the Braves was also pitching a shutout into the thirteenth. Think about the magnitude of that. Both pitchers kept going out there to battle the other, inning after inning, neither of them giving an inch. That's something that will *never* happen again.

It was an inspiring effort by two gamers—until that thirteenth inning. I guess that's why they say 13 is an unlucky number.

An error by Don Hoak in the bottom of the thirteenth with the Braves at the plate ended the perfect game bid by Haddix. At least he still had the no-hitter....

A sacrifice bunt moved the runner over to second. Hank Aaron was intentionally walked, which brought Joe Adcock to the plate.

Harvey had one of the worst nicknames I've ever heard: "Kitten."

Do I have to tell you the end of the story?

Three-run homer (that was changed to a double after Adrock passed Aaron on the bases) for a Braves win—and Haddix loses the no-hitter, the shutout, and the game in one pitch. After all that brilliant pitching!

It's sad for me to think about Haddix even after all this time. He doesn't get credit for anything but an extra-inning loss. He pitched a perfect game through nine—hell, he was perfect through 12. But his team didn't win. His Pirate teammates just couldn't push a run across.

Rules are rules.

When Haddix was asked about his historic outing, he said, "All I know is we lost. What's so historic about that?" I love this guy.

Chris Chambliss Sends New York to the World Series

If you're going to write a book about the most outrageous plays ever on a baseball field, you have to talk to as many people as possible—players, umpires, managers, coaches, vendors, broadcasters, and fans.

They've all seen something unbelievable. Everybody's perspective counts! Whenever I posed the simple question, "What's the craziest play you've ever seen?" to a guy who'd been around the game a while, I'd get a response like "Get back to me on that one," or "I gotta think about it."

But Willie Randolph didn't need any time to reflect.

He knew the instant I asked him what his answer would be. So was it Reggie Jackson sticking his butt out to intentionally get hit in the 1978 World Series? Or was it Roger Clemens throwing the business end of a bat at Mike Piazza in the Subway Series of 2000? Tommy John's three errors on one play? Nope! Even though he saw each of those with his own two eyes, Willie didn't even hesitate when he said it was Chris Chambliss' game-winning homer against the Kansas City Royals that put the Yankees into the 1976 World Series.

> Chambliss is currently the hitting coach for the Triple A Richmond Braves.

"I was only 22 years old," Willie said. "When he hit it, I don't know why, but when I saw all the people running onto the field—in those days, there wasn't any security keeping people from jumping over the fences—all I could think about was that rule that said even if you hit a home run, you still have to touch all the bases. So I was running out there elbowing people and pushing people away from Chris because I wanted to make sure he got all the way around the bases in one piece. I got halfway to second base and turned around because it was too dangerous out there. Crazy! Someone tried to grab my hat and, back then, I had the big Afro workin' and I could feel a handful of my hair ripping out of my head while the guy was yanking off my hat.

Chris Chambliss is mobbed by fans after his walk-off home run in the 1976 ALCS.

"So now I'm running back to the dugout and I was looking for my dad, who came to the game. He was trying to get down to the field to see me, but a security guy stopped him and had him in a headlock. Like a choke hold. I was screaming at the security guy to let him go but there was so much confusion and noise he didn't understand what I meant. Finally I got close enough to yell at the guy, 'That's my father, let him go!' So I grab him, and we sneak back down through the dugout to the clubhouse and drank lots of champagne. No big deal."

It must have been scary down on the field. I was scared just watching it on TV. There's Chambliss running the bases, trying to keep his batting helmet on and knocking fans over like they were bowling pins. Even though the Yankees were playing at home and the fans were jumping on the field to celebrate, as a player, you have no idea what their motives are. Imagine a mass of delirious people running at you and all you're trying to do is make it back to home plate after hitting a home run. But it had been about 12 years since Yankee fans had anything to celebrate and I guess they were just letting loose!

Ronald Reagan, Meet Bo Jackson

On Opening Day, it's tradition for the president of the United States to throw out the first pitch of the season. Sometimes, if you're a lucky broadcaster, the president might even stop by for a half-inning chat, but that doesn't happen too often and it's always pretty superficial. I don't think anybody in Washington wants the president going off the cuff, answering questions from some baseball announcer.

Ronald Reagan, however, came from Hollywood and had a life that was as diverse as one could ever live. True to his personality, when President Reagan walked into the broadcast booth at the 1989 All-Star Game in Anaheim, he decided he'd stay for an inning or so. It was no shock to the network that Reagan, a former broadcaster himself, was on the air when Bo Jackson led off the game for the American League. The real shocker came when Bo went yard to deep center field…and President Reagan made the home-run call!

Usually when someone is visiting the booth, they stop talking and let the pros talk if something worth talking about is happening on the field. But President Reagan was in mid-sentence when Bo swung, and he was having so much fun he decided to call the home run himself. And why wouldn't he feel comfortable doing so? He was a sports announcer in his early years, even calling Chicago Cubs games from 1933 to 1936. It was a great time to be in the booth, as Wade Boggs followed Bo's blast with one of his own.

So to this day, the only TV account of Bo Jackson's home run in the 1989 All-Star Game is a call made by the president of the United States. It was a special night for Bo: he robbed Pedro Guerrero of a home run, hit a home run himself that traveled 448 feet, and had his home run called by a some guy who used to be in the movies.

Joe Nuxhall Makes Debuts at 15

In 1944, we as a country were in the middle of World War II. Many major-league players were fighting overseas. Many grown men didn't come home. Kids in school were afraid they'd be drafted.

The Cincinnati Reds had a serious shortage of players, so on June 10 of that year, Joe Nuxhall made his debut. His first appearance wasn't a great one—he came in to pitch the ninth inning of a 13–0 ballgame against Stan Musial and the Cardinals and gave up five runs—but what was memorable was Nuxhall's age: he was just 15 years old, making him, to this day, the youngest player in MLB history.

Now, I know we've had a lot of young men debut in the big leagues at early ages, but they've been 18 years old or close to 18. Dwight Gooden, Ken Griffey Jr., and Bob Feller come to mind. But Nuxhall was just 15—he should have been studying chemistry or preparing for a test in high school, not pitching at Crosley Field! I don't know if I'd have been able to do it, because those hitters weren't going to show any mercy against Joe just because he was a kid—literally!—in his first big-league game.

I don't know what would honestly compel a manager to throw him into that situation, but I guess for Joe it was all good, since it launched his career in baseball, albeit a bit prematurely. The Ol' Left-Hander wound up broadcasting games for the Reds for almost 40 years and passed away in 2007.

Good work, kid.

CHAPTER NINE

Anger Management

Phil Wellman Goes Berserk

Every baseball fan knows the masters of the ejection: Earl Weaver, with his hat turned sideways so that he could get closer to the umpire's face and spit more tobacco juice on him; Billy Martin, with arms flailing and curse words flying; and Lou Piniella, who actually became more famous after he memorably tossed a base into the outfield.

But all of those repeat offenders pale in comparison to Phil Wellman, minor-league manager of the Mississippi Braves.

On June 1, 2007, Wellman thought his pitchers were getting squeezed, only to watch the strike zone double in size when his batters were at the plate. This made him more than just a little upset, and he decided to let the umpires know about it.

> **Wellman is still the manager of the Mississippi Braves.**

It's technically illegal to argue balls and strikes, so Wellman was ejected pretty quickly. But he was just getting warmed up, and that's when the wackiness started.

After bumping the home-plate umpire, Wellman took a page out of Martin's playbook and covered home plate with dirt. When the dish was totally covered and neatly groomed, Phil drew an outline of a new home plate that was twice as big as the real thing. After discussing his handiwork with the home-plate umpire, Wellman figured he wasn't getting through to the guy and turned his attention to the third-base umpire. That didn't work any better, so Wellman decided to steal one of Piniella's moves—he ripped the third-base bag out of the ground, then walked out to shallow center field and tossed it as far as he could!

Phil Wellman punched his ticket for the Crazy Manager Hall of Fame after this tirade in 2007.

For most managers, the ejection, the chest bumping, the dirt piling, and the base throwing would've been enough for one day. But Phil wasn't done yet. He began to crawl back toward the infield on his belly until he reached the back of the pitcher's mound, where he grabbed the rosin bag and then, pretending it was a grenade, acted like he was pulling the pin out of it and launched it toward home plate! A former ballplayer himself, Wellman had perfect aim and the rosin bag landed right at the feet of the umpire, who by then must have known he was seeing one of the greatest tirades of all time.

Just for good measure, Wellman grabbed both the second-base bag and the bag he'd already thrown and took them with him as he left the field. But before he left, he stopped and took a bow, signifying the end of a once-in-a-lifetime performance.

Wellman was fined and suspended for his outburst, of course, and I'm sure the Braves organization had some stern words for him as well. But Wellman still manages in their system today, so you gotta figure he puts as much passion into managing as he does into being ejected. And he seems like the type of guy I would have loved to play for.

Lou Piniella Gets Tossed and Tosses Third Base

When Lou Piniella played for the Yankees back in the wild and crazy 1970s, everyone thought he played with a lot of heart…and a lot of hair, as he sported a full head of locks that would make his cap fly off whenever he ran around the bases.

I knew that Lou would make a great manager because he's always been a student of the game. He managed the Reds to the 1990 World Series and later took the Seattle Mariners from the outhouse to the penthouse in one year! He went on to revamp the Rays' farm system and is now the Cubs' manager and the face of their franchise.

However, I also believed that one day Lou might end up having a stroke right on the field—that man gets red in the face when he gets angry!

One of his most memorable outbursts came on August 21, 1990. Lou's Reds were taking on the Cubs in Cincinnati when All-Star shortstop Barry Larkin was called out at first on a bang-bang play. Piniella jumped out of the dugout and started arguing with first-base umpire Dutch Rennert.

Not feeling satisfied after he'd had his say, Lou threw his hat on the ground, at which point Rennert tossed him from the game. But Sweet Lou was still not feeling very sweet—he bent down, ripped the first-base bag out of the ground, and tossed it toward right field! And just in case Rennert didn't get the message, Lou picked it up and tossed it again! The crowd was delighted. Rennert and the folks at Major League Baseball were not.

That tirade became a signature moment in Lou's managing career, and he got the last laugh when his commercial for Aquafina water came out in 2008. In the ad, a call doesn't go Lou's way and he runs out of the dugout and tells the umpire…that he's "doing a good job" and that he should "say hello to the missus."

If there's a lesson to be learned here, I guess it's this: get mad, throw your cap, heave first base into right field, and then get paid to do a national commercial!

Tommy Lasorda Attacks the Phillie Phanatic

Breaking news: Tommy Lasorda is not a fan of the Phillie Phanatic.

Back in August 1988, the legendary Dodgers manager took bleeding Dodger Blue to new Psycho heights when he actually got into a physical altercation with the Phillies' mascot right on the field, during the middle of a game!

Now, anyone who knows Tommy knows that he doesn't find the "desecration" of anything to do with the Dodgers funny. He takes it all pretty seriously. I mean *really* seriously. Tommy gets an

A for effort as far as his passion for the Dodgers goes, that's for sure.

So on this day, the Phanatic came out during the game to do his usual crowd-pleasing act, only this time he had a prop with him: a big, fat doll dressed in a Dodgers uniform with "Lasorda" written on the back!

Tommy probably could've handled that, but then the Phanantic started stomping on the doll!

Needless to say, at that point Tommy had seen enough and just charged out of the dugout and wrestled the doll away from Dave Raymond, the guy inside the Phanatic costume. In the end, the Phanatic was pinned on the ground by Lasorda, who got a few punches in for good measure.

But the more Lasorda screamed and steamed, the further Raymond went in provoking him. Dave sometimes went over the edge, but he never forgot the "importance of our fans." He loved to tweak Tommy because he knew Tommy didn't like it.

"I was just trying to have some fun," Raymond said afterward.

"He didn't need to stomp on the doll. This wasn't entertainment. He was teaching the kids violence," Lasorda said.

Hey, lesson to mascots: don't mess with Lasorda—even if you are just having "fun." Not when it comes to Dodger Blue.

Lloyd McClendon Steals a Base

Managers scream and yell. They rant and rave. They kick dirt. They break water coolers and tear up locker rooms. But rarely do they take souvenirs home with them after an argument.

Pirates manager Lloyd McClendon takes his base and goes home after getting tossed from a game in 2001.

Back on June 26, 2001, the Pirates were playing the Milwaukee Brewers when a call at first base went against Pittsburgh, or so said first-base umpire Rick Reed.

The Pirates' manager at the time, Lloyd McClendon, is a rather civilized guy. He didn't yell and scream or kick dirt. He didn't take

193

a bat and destroy the dugout. He didn't throw things in his office. He just decided that there was only one way to avoid another call at first base going against his team.

So, rather than imitate Lou Piniella, McClendon did him one better.

Lloyd actually walked onto the field, argued the call, and walked off the field after his ejection in Pittsburgh—with first base tucked neatly under his arm. He then threw the base into the dugout and headed down the tunnel without batting an eyelash or turning around.

Lloyd is now the hitting coach for the Detroit Tigers.

Usually, when a manager gets mad enough to bend down and dislodge a base from its rightful home, he'll toss it somewhere—it adds to the effect. Never have I seen a guy just take a base home with him, like paperwork from a job or homework from school after a hard day's work.

The umpires didn't even bother to retrieve the base. They just found a replacement and allowed that one to rest quietly on the dugout floor where McClendon left it. I guess Lloyd figured he didn't steal many bases as a player, so he might as well get one as a manager.

Lloyd was one of the few kids from a Little League World Series to make it to the big leagues. He just had the type of raw talent that put him head and shoulders above other kids. In fact, he once homered five times in a row, so you might say that even back then Lloyd had an affinity for collecting bases—RBIs, that is.

Hal McRae Has Seen Enough

We've all seen managers go a little nuts during interviews with reporters; sometimes the questions just keep coming and they're not the ones any manager wants to hear. Sometimes the questions have already been answered, or they make no sense, or they're designed to make the manager or his players look bad. Every manager has to find his own way to deal with the insanity of it all, but sometimes they just snap.

Such was the case with Kansas City Royals manager Hal McRae one day in his office after a tough loss early in the 1993 season. Always known for being a good guy and for being available to the media, McRae had been asked what he thought was a stupid question and snapped in grand style. He got up from his desk and he went to work redecorating his office. By the time he was done, there wasn't anything left on his desk that wasn't nailed down. Files, papers, pencils, and even a telephone went flying around the office! Unfortunately for Hal, one of those objects bounced off the face of one of the beat reporters and drew a little blood.

It was unfortunate because Hal was not a bad guy. He wasn't trying to hurt anybody. But he had to face the music once the tantrum was over and the reporter emerged bloody and bruised. In fact, the tantrum only became legendary because somebody else videotaped the whole thing. Otherwise, it would have been one of the many blowups that happen every year that nobody ever hears about.

I guess it just proves that the pen is mightier than the sword…or phone.

CHAPTER TEN

Fun at the Ol' Ballpark

Larry Walker Bats Right-Handed

Randy Johnson has won five Cy Young Awards in his career. In 1997, he went 20–4, and at that season's All-Star Game, all 6'10" of him scared the daylights out of almost every hitter he faced. Larry Walker was no exception.

The left-handed Walker came to the plate and the lefty Johnson uncorked a pitch that sailed so far over Walker's head, everyone had a good laugh. But then Walker got to thinking, *What if that pitch had hit me?*

I'm sure he had flashbacks to the confrontation Johnson had with John Kruk back in the 1993 All-Star Game. That one ended in a humorous strikeout for Kruk. So Walker put on his own comedy act that night for the fans. He figured he had no chance of hitting The Big Unit left-handed, so why not go down swinging righty?

Larry Walker was a five-time All-Star and won the NL MVP Award in 1997.

When Walker jumped to the other side of the plate and then turned his batting helmet around backward, the place went crazy with laughter. It was truly one of the classic All-Star moments of all time and, like many of the stories in this book, it's one of those moments that reminds people why they love the game of baseball.

On top of the laughs he got, the scheme also worked for the National League team because Walker ended up drawing a walk.

No, this photo is not backward; Larry Walker went right-handed against Randy Johnson at the 1997 All-Star Game.

Walker and Johnson were like a comedy team at that point. Walker's helmet act wouldn't have been funny if Johnson hadn't played along; Johnson, on the other hand, would have been just another tall, lanky, dominating lefty if Walker hadn't pulled his stunt. It turned out to be a way better option than asking to be pinch-hit for!

Bobby Valentine Goes Incognito

Bobby Valentine and trouble go together like Laurel and Hardy, Lindsay Lohan and nightclubs, or me and Fox Sports. Back in the heat of a pennant race in 1999, Bobby V got into a heated argument during the twelfth inning of a game between the Blue Jays and the Mets over a call that went against New York catcher Mike Piazza. While everyone forgot what the heck the whole thing was about, nobody could forget Valentine's reaction after the umpire tossed him from the game. Rather than kicking dirt, emptying the bat rack, tossing stuff onto the field, or picking up and heaving a base or two into the outfield, Valentine did as he was told—he left the game.

But Major League Baseball has a little rule called Rule 4.07. It basically states that once you've been ejected from a game by an umpire, you can't—duh!—come back. Nobody in their right mind has ever even attempted to fight this rule. That's because even though the manager may have gotten himself kicked out of a game, that doesn't mean he's going to stop managing that game. Everybody knows he'll just watch the game on TV in the clubhouse and send all the important decisions to the "acting" manager through one of the batboys.

But that wasn't good enough for Bobby V.

Bobby decided that managing from the clubhouse wasn't close enough to the action, so he returned to the dugout—only looking a little different this time around. It wasn't long before the cameras from the Mets' local television network figured out that something wasn't quite right. They realized during the end of the inning that there was a guy in the dugout wearing a black Mets T-shirt, sunglasses, and a really bad fake mustache. By then, everyone knew who it was, and I thought the stunt was pretty funny. But Katy Feeney and the rest of the higher-ups at the MLB offices didn't find it so amusing. That disguise might just be the most expensive costume in baseball history—as it cost Bobby V $5,000 in fines and eventually helped him punch a one-way ticket to managing in Japan.

Bobby is in his second stint as manager of the Chiba Lotte Marines.

I think the gag was great for baseball because it showed managers were human, that they have a sense of humor even after throwing a temper tantrum. The punishment for what Bobby V did was much harsher than what others have received.

That prank may never be duplicated, mostly because no manager want to pay the $5,000, but also because there's only one Bobby Valentine.

Rick Dempsey Gets Wet

Rick Dempsey's dad had been a vaude-ville actor, and his mother was a Broadway star. A great catcher in his own right, Rick led the Baltimore Orioles to greatness, but nevertheless loved to clown around during rain delays and in the clubhouse before and after games.

The Orioles were always in the middle of something unusual, whether it was the 1969 World Series when they were on the wrong end of some great plays, or the numerous ejections of their firebrand manager, Earl Weaver. But they were perennial contenders and for good reason. The leader of the 1980s Baltimore teams was their Hall of Fame shortstop, Cal Ripken Jr. But every team needs a good catcher, and the O's were lucky to have a great catcher in Rick Dempsey.

Rick should be remembered for great plays, clutch hits, and the way he handled the pitching staff. He knew how to call a game, whether he was catching Hall of Famer Jim Palmer or Tippy Martinez, and that experience eventually led him to become an analyst for MASN after he retired.

> Rick was the MVP of the 1983 World Series.

But Rick is comically remembered for one incident in 1977. The O's were playing the Red Sox at Fenway Park when Mother Nature forced the game to wait a few hours. Dempsey had time on his hands, and that spelled trouble. Or did it spell F-U-N?

During one of the many torrential rainstorms that hit New England in the summertime at odd moments, Dempsey decided to see if the crowd thought he measured up in theatrics to his mom and dad.

Rick stuffed his shirt with towels and did a Babe Ruth imitation. As if that wasn't enough, for a curtain call he went a bit further, and that's what got him into this book.

After the Babe Ruth schtick, Dempsey decided it'd be great fun if the fans could watch him slide across the rain-soaked tarp! Dempsey raced across the tarp on the field and slid clear across it like a five-year-old on a water slide. The fans loved it! Suddenly, the organist started playing "Raindrops Keep Fallin' on My Head" from the hit movie *Butch Cassidy and the Sundance Kid*.

Orioles catcher Rick Dempsey, also known as the master of rain delay theater.

What was a fan and PR disaster of a game turned into a treat for both Sox and Orioles fans as they got to see Dempsey playing in the rain like a big kid. Sometimes the part of a ballgame you remember doesn't happen in the game at all.

Tic-Tac-Toe

I think everybody knows that I loved playing baseball and tried to have as much fun as I could before and after the game, but during the game I was usually so nervous I didn't even know what was going on around me. One year while I was playing in Chicago, I had to do something to make things a little more fun. Then I had a conversation with Rusty Kuntz. He was the first-base coach for the Mariners at the time and I was playing first base for the White Sox.

He said that he used to break things up by playing tic-tac-toe with other players…on the field, during the game! He definitely told the wrong guy if he thought his secret would be safe and stored in the minor leagues somewhere. I tried it out the next game and kept right on doing it.

While the pitcher was taking his final warm-up tosses right before the game started, I would draw a big tic-tac-toe game right inside the foul line. Considering our team was 25 games out of first place at the time and we were all looking for something to have fun with, it worked out pretty well. I was undefeated!

I would put my X in at the top of the first and then wait for the opposing first baseman to take his position at the bottom of the inning. Usually when I came back out, my opponent had made his move and the game was on!

I always got advice on the move I was going to make from umpires, first-base coaches, and even fans who were high enough up to see what I was doing. Toward the end I'd always put two X's in on my final move for the victory. Sometimes the other players were confused and didn't realize how I beat them!

Some people around the game didn't think it was so funny. They figured I wasn't concentrating on the game or I was messing with the integrity of baseball. I didn't care because I had the blessing of my manager, Jeff Torborg, who was always a stickler about integrity. The two owners of the White Sox used to laugh about it from their luxury box upstairs.

Sometimes I'd get thrown a change-up from other players— Kent Hrbek wanted to play hangman one night after tic-tac-toe. I beat him at his own game. After getting a head and a few body parts because of some bad guesses, I decided to guess the letter P. Hrbek's word was a four-letter word, and knowing him, I was a little afraid of what the word might be. But when I returned the word looked like this: P_ _P.

Game over. Yep, POOP!

I became a league-wide legend!

Sometimes I'd write notes in the dirt just to see if I'd get an answer. Once when I was playing second base, I asked opposing second baseman Harold Reynolds if he could get to a ball at a certain spot. I wrote, "Can you get to this ball?" and then drew a long line in the dirt up the middle and behind second base. Two innings later he ranged far to his right, snagged a grounder, and threw out my teammate Greg Walker. It was the type of play that earned him a Gold Glove for his outstanding defensive play at second. When I returned for the top of the next inning, I got my answer written in the dirt. It simply read: "Yes."

Most people would consider this behavior a little crazy and certainly out of the norm. I guess that's why it makes the book. I look at times like that and wonder why they don't happen more often.

Don't you?

Eric Gregg Gets a Delivery

Umpires have the worst job in all of sports. It always amazes me when people criticize them as if umpires and referees don't take pride in what they do. I have news for those people: umpires want to do their job well as much as the players do. It's their big leagues too, and even though sometimes an umpire might get a little confrontational, so do the players. The bottom line is that these guys are ridiculously good at what they do. How many times do you see a play at first base and you'd swear the guy was safe, but the umpire rings him up? Then you get to check the replay from four different angles, in slow motion, and on the third one you finally realize the umpire's call was correct. They don't get to watch the play again in slow motion and they only get to see the play from one angle—and they have to make that call immediately! Trust me, they're good at what they do.

Meanwhile, they have to do their job with guys jawing at them all the time. The hitter thought that ball was outside, the pitcher thinks he's getting squeezed, the managers don't like anything they do, and the fans want to kill them. The umpire can't win. Either he does a good job and nobody notices, or he screws up a call and everyone jumps on his back.

Umpire Eric Gregg was a great guy, but his love of food contributed to his poor health.

But sometimes a lighter moment comes along that puts the entire game of baseball into perspective. After all, the game is just that—a kid's game.

Ron Luciano was one guy who loved to test the limits of the umpire-player relationship. One moment he'd be joking around with a player and the next moment he'd be breaking out his famous "shoot 'em down" sign at first base to call a player out.

Eric Gregg was another umpire who took his job seriously but also found the fun in the game. Nicknamed "The Plump Ump,"

Gregg was indeed a big man. Listed at 325 pounds, even he admitted that he was usually closer to 400.

Back in 1988, Gregg was the third-base umpire at Busch Stadium and one of the players decided to have a little fun at his expense. In between innings, Gregg turned around and suddenly noticed something odd about third base. An object was sitting there that wasn't supposed to be there. When he went over to check it out, he burst out laughing. Somebody had left him a hamburger!

When he was hired in 1975, Gregg was just the third African American umpire in league history.

It was a prank that nobody was willing to own up to, but Gregg figured there was no sense in wasting a perfectly good burger. Instead of getting angry, he smiled and held the hamburger up to the cameras—and then he ate it!

It was one of the funniest moments ever and it showed just how human the guys in blue really are.

Sadly, Eric Gregg is no longer with us. He passed away after a stroke in 2006. But he was an accomplished and very likable umpire who worked the 1989 World Series and was behind the plate for two no-hitters during his career. His love of the game is still missed today.

Don Mattingly Loves Popcorn

I love popcorn. Who doesn't? I eat popcorn at the movies like I think somebody's going to take it away from me. I get the huge bucket that costs like $17, and trust me, I get those free refills they offer, too.

But I like eating popcorn while I'm sitting at the movies, not after taking it from some kid's bucket in the stands while I'm on the field playing a baseball game!

Only a guy like Don Mattingly could get away with stealing a kid's popcorn at a game and look good doing it. Donnie's a great guy, and this was one of the more spontaneous and playful moments I've ever seen.

Everything Don Mattingly did was fluid and effortless, from his MVP swing to the way he dealt with fans, the media, and other players. The guy is class all the way. Mark my words, Don will be a manager someday soon. Right now he's just biding his time under the tutelage of Joe Torre in the Dodgers' dugout. But when he wants it, he'll have his pick of any job he wants in the major leagues.

But this moment happened back during his playing days. One day during the lean years at Yankee Stadium, Mattingly followed a pop-up into foul ground and watched it land in the stands.

The ball landed about 20 rows back and Don saw this kid staring up at him with a big bucket of popcorn in his lap. After a brief stare-down contest, Mattingly asked the kid if he could have a handful. It was like that old Coca-Cola commercial with Mean Joe Greene, where the kid stands in awe of his sports idol.

So Mattingly dipped into the kid's popcorn bucket and grabbed himself a snack. But what most fans don't know is that after the inning was over, Mattingly came back and gave the kid an autographed baseball and thanked him for the popcorn. He told me that when he asked the kid if he could have some, the kid just stared at him, scared to death. He felt bad so he brought over the ball as a thank-you.

Now the hitting coach for the Dodgers, Mattingly has a lot more than eating popcorn on his mind. But I bet if he got the chance, he'd do it again.

In 1985, I pulled the same trick. I was playing second base for Boston and we were in Seattle. I guess the big difference was that the kid didn't idolize me and, truth be told, he didn't even know I was stealing his popcorn! He was watching the foul ball go over his head and I just saw an opportunity to do something offbeat. I grabbed a handful and then took off back to my position at second base.

Papelbon Auditions for *Riverdance*

The Red Sox had just won their second ALCS in three years. Jonathan Papelbon was on the mound in Boston for the clinching out in Game 7. So he did what anybody would have done. After throwing the final pitch, he screamed like a teenager, tore his hat from his head, and jumped for the heavens. He hugged his teammates, drank champagne, and then he did something he should not have done.

Let's call it Papelbon's audition for the touring company of *Riverdance*.

Yes, *Riverdance*, as in the Irish step dancers. He had done it before, and he told Jason Varitek, Kevin Youkilis, and other teammates that if the Sox went to the World Series he'd do it again right on the field. Everybody pleaded with him not to. But clad in his champagne-drenched T-shirt, Papelbon did that dance in front of everyone on national television, bringing new meaning to the phrase "postgame celebration."

Was this a genuine display of enthusiasm? Yes. Was it cool? Not so much.

Jonathan Papelbon "dances" after Boston won Game 7 of the 2007 ALCS against the Indians.

It's hard to describe how bad Papelbon's dancing was to someone who didn't see it. The only thing I can compare it to is the pitiful dancing that Mark Madsen did during the victory parade in L.A. after the Lakers won the NBA championship in 2001. That was ugly. Any tall, gangly white guy should have a permanent restraining order keeping him at least 500 feet from a dance floor at all times.

But this moment was 100 percent Papelbon. He's a workhorse on the mound who's full of energy and emotion. He had a great year for the Sox and was as automatic as any closer could be, saving 37 games that year. So it's hard to deny a young kid the chance to dance a little after clinching a trip to the World Series. Who knows, maybe he'll decide to take dancing lessons, or compete on *Dancing with the Stars*!

And Papelbon's outburst is one of the great things about baseball. Any championship, whether it's in Little League or the major leagues, deserves to be celebrated. The injuries and win streaks, the high fives and bruised egos, the fears and the fights, the home runs and double plays—it all becomes a dizzying blur. So when you finally climb that mountain, maybe you should just go ahead and dance a little.

Even if you dance like Papelbon.

Jimmy Piersall's Water Pistol

How can I do a book like this without Jimmy Piersall in it? But how do you pick just one of the off-the-wall things he did? Jimmy was known to have stirred the pot quite a few times. He once took a curtain call after a home run—on the road. He wore a wig that made him look like the fifth shaggy-haired member of the Beatles during a ballgame. He was a classic example of a guy whose mind and personality never let his incredible talent really break through.

But one of Piersall's pranks is a classic that never made it to the hit movie *Fear Strikes Out*, the cinematic version of Jimmy's life story. It happened back on July 16, 1952.

The box score that day noted that Jimmy Piersall struck out in the second inning and was subsequently ejected.

But like many box scores, it doesn't tell the whole story. What's important here is *why* Piersall was ejected.

Before his at-bat, Piersall whipped a water pistol out of his back pocket and squirted it a few times in honor of his teammate Milt Bolling's home run. Then, after striking out, he promptly left the field of play, climbed into the left-field stands, and started heckling the umpire! What else could the umpires do? Of course they tossed him.

The water pistol stunt was the one that eventually led to Piersall seeking treatment for his bipolar disorder, an illness that wasn't diagnosed correctly at the time. He went on to have a successful career in the broadcast booth, and he accompanied the 2004 World Series champion Red Sox during their celebratory trip to the White House.

Harry Being Harry

Back when I was playing in Triple A, I dreamt of the day I might get called up to the big leagues. I certainly wasn't a sure-fire prospect who had one of those "can't miss" tags on me. My dream of making it up to "the show" was just that—a dream. (As a side note, nobody in the majors ever calls it "the show"—only minor-league guys who haven't been there yet call the big leagues "the show.") Sure, there were guys I played against—like Darryl Strawberry—and guys I played with—like Roger Clemens—who I knew were going to make it big, but I wasn't one of 'em.

I had another dream back in those days: that one day I'd make it to the show—I mean, the big leagues—and that broadcasting legend Harry Caray would have a reason to announce my name.

During the day, most guys were into the soap operas on daytime TV. They'd run around asking each other, "What are Luke and Laura going to do today?" I didn't like the soaps much, so I was tuned into a Cubs game, listening to Harry and Steve Stone.

What a piece of work Harry was—he could get away with saying almost anything he wanted and often did. I think almost everybody has a favorite story about Harry. I remember one day when Harry was broadcasting the game from out in the bleachers. He usually had a cooler out there with him, and of course he used to be a pitch man for Budweiser beer, so draw your own conclusions on what beverage he was drinking that day.

This was back when the Cubs had Jody Davis catching and Ron Cey playing third base. So one of the opposing hitters strikes out, and Davis starts throwing it around the horn. But I guess Harry wasn't 100 percent focused on the game because he said, "Here comes the 3–2 pitch….fastball and a line shot down to Cey at third and he makes the play! Boy, he snagged that one out of the air and prevented a sure double down the line!"

I was rolling on the floor laughing but it must have been even harder for Stone to keep a straight face. He said, "Uh, no, Harry, that was a swinging strike three and Jody was just tossing the ball around the horn." It was a classic Harry moment.

I asked Stoney for one of his favorite Harry stories, and he told me about the time they spoke to President Reagan from the broadcast booth.

"When Harry Caray came back to the Cubs after recovering from a serious stroke, he was welcomed with open arms by the mayor and the entire Cubs team. Everyone wanted to wish him well, so much so that a phone call came to the booth," Stone recalls.

"Harry, this is President Reagan," said the voice through the speaker phone. "I just wanted to welcome you back. The Cubs need you, the baseball world needs you, and the country needs you. You're great for baseball."

"Thank you, Mr. President," Harry said, still looking down at the game in progress.

"Well, the president went on and I clearly heard him talking about his wife Nancy and about Chicago and his memories of Illinois and certain things he and Harry had in common," Stone continued, "when all of a sudden, right in the middle of his sentence, Harry says, 'Mr. President, Bob Dernier just singled and I've got to let you go!' And then Harry hung up! He didn't say good-bye. Never in my life have I ever seen anyone speak so long to a president, much less literally hang up on one! But that was Harry."

It took a long time before I got the thrill of having Harry announce my name. I made it to the big leagues in 1985, but playing for the Red Sox in the American League kept me away from Harry and his Cubs. I didn't cross paths with him until a few years later when I was playing for the White Sox and we used to play the Cubs in the "Crosstown Classic" (that was long before the days of interleague play). That game was also the one in which I played all nine positions in one game. It was great! Harry called me by three different first names that day, and during my five seasons in Chicago we never lost to the Cubs.

Later I ran into Harry at an awards dinner and was shocked that he remembered my name. I was just a third-year player, a nobody and certainly not someone Harry Caray should have remembered. But before the dinner he walked right up to me and said, "There's Steve Lyons, how ya doing Steve?"

Wow! I felt like I was in the show!

I've Been Traded Where?

When you're a rookie, people treat you like you're a little kid—you should be seen and not heard. It's not always like that today, with the $6 million signing bonuses and guaranteed major-league contracts given to high draft choices before they even play in one professional game. A lot of the young guys today come up to the big leagues thinking they know everything and don't have to listen to anybody else. That's not true of all young kids; I never got that impression from Kyle Kendrick of the Phillies. He came up for his rookie year in the middle of the pennant race in 2007, was thrown right into the fire, and won 10 games. A lot of people said the job Kendrick did was one of the main reasons the Phillies got into the playoffs that year. To me, he seemed like one of those guys who wanted to learn and get better, kept his mouth shut, and just pitched.

So is that a guy you'd want to trade the following spring training? Sure, it's happened before; a team gets offered a deal that's too good to pass up, but it involves a young player who has had some early success. The organization has to make a tough decision.

And that's what assistant general manager Ruben Amaro Jr. and Phillies manager Charlie Manuel told Kendrick in spring of 2008. They said he had been traded to Japan for a fictional player named Kobayashi Iwamura. Kendrick was stunned. His heart sank and his head was spinning. "So many things went through my head," he said. "I just bought a new car—what was I going to do with that in Japan? I won 10 games, why would they trade me?"

Kendrick was living near Seattle and he figured at the very least he'd be able to stop at home for a day or two to get his affairs together and clear his head.

"No," Amaro Jr. told him. "They want you there tomorrow." So in comes the traveling secretary with the flight information, and Kendrick's flight didn't even connect in Seattle. The young pitcher staggered out of Manuel's office and quietly went to his locker to grab his cell phone. His first call was to his agent to try and understand what was going on. But his agent told him it was a great opportunity to make a lot of money and not to worry about it. Then he told some of his teammates, including Brett Myers, Pat Burrell, and others. They were all in disbelief.

Next came the impromptu press conference with Amaro Jr. telling the media the front office made the move to "take their team to the next level."

When Kendrick got his chance to speak, he was able to muster a sense of humor. "Do they have good food over there?" he asked.

A few questions into the press conference, Myers butted in with an opinion of his own. "You know what I think about this whole thing, don't you?" said Myers. "I think you've been Punk'd!"

The relief on Kendrick's face was something everybody could see. The media members were laughing hysterically and Kendrick finally took a deep breath, knowing he'd been tricked but happy that he was staying put.

It turned out almost everybody was in on the prank. There was a lot of planning that went into this, from Amaro Jr. and Manuel all the way to the beat reporters. Myers knew, the traveling secretary knew, Kendrick's agent knew, half the team knew—but Kendrick didn't.

Kendrick finished fifth in the Rookie of the Year voting in 2007.

Teammates Pedro Feliz and Shane Victorino both said he handled himself well. "Who knows how I would have reacted," said Victorino. "I don't think you can get traded to Japan, but you're not thinking about that when somebody walks up and tells you that you've just been traded. I don't know if I would have handled it as well."

After just a half a year in the big leagues, Kendrick certainly wasn't one of those rookies who thought he knew it all, but he was quickly becoming one of those guys who had seen it all.

He just never acted that way.

David Wells Wears the Babe's Cap!

On June 28, 1997, David Wells was getting ready to make a start in Yankee Stadium and something was just a little off. Now with Boomer, sometimes it's a little hard to pinpoint exactly what qualifies as just a little "off." David's got a big personality and an even bigger waistline, and he's always talkin' and playing around. But he did do his job; heck, he won 239 games in the big leagues.

But this day was different, even for him. This day, Wells thought it would be cool to honor one of his boyhood idols in a way that nobody had ever tried before. Wells loved Babe Ruth and all the things the Babe stood for—the talent, the carousing, and the attention he demanded. Boomer even wanted to wear Babe's No. 3 when he joined the Yankees, but since that number is retired, Boomer chose No. 33 instead. On this day, Wells decided to do something extra special to pay tribute to one of his heroes. He decided to wear Ruth's hat instead, and not just one of those throwback caps you can buy at the gift shop—he wore one of Babe's actual caps!

Boomer has two World Series rings and was the MVP of the 1998 ALCS.

Wells had just purchased a 1934 vintage cap at an auction for $35,000. That's a ton of money for a cap, but not when you're making Boomer's salary. I thought it was cool because Wells is a genuine guy and he really wanted to wear it to honor the Babe during a game. And wear it he did!

The umpires, buzzkills that they are, were so touched by David's love for the Babe…that they made him take off the hat! They told Yankees manager Joe Torre to have David take it off for "failure to conform to the uniform rules." But Boomer did get away with it for a few pitches.

That hat used to conform to the uniform code, but time marches on and things change. It still had the classic NY on the front in white and the hat itself was blue— just a slightly different shade of blue. And it was a little snug on Wells' head, the same way hats were back in the old days.

Does David Wells' cap look funny to you? It should—it was 63 years old!

It was definitely a nice gesture on David's part as both his cap and stomach honored the Babe that day. I still applaud Boomer for giving it a whirl. After all, baseball needs guys like Boomer to keep things fun.

By the way, it didn't matter which cap Wells wore that day, as he blew a 3–0 lead against Cleveland and the Indians ended up winning the game 12–8.

Eddie Gaedel Pinch-Hits

Many years ago, kids dreamed of playing in the major leagues, or if they were really desperate, running away and joining the circus. Heck, I've heard former Yankees tell me they felt like they had fulfilled both those dreams playing for George Steinbrenner and Billy Martin.

But Bill Veeck is the one who really did his best to combine the two: on August 19, 1951, Bill had little person Eddie Gaedel take an at-bat for his St. Louis Browns, making Eddie the smallest pinch-hitter of all time.

Gaedel was just 3'7" and remarkably drew a walk in his only big-league at-bat. Of course he drew a walk—they said his strike zone was only an inch-and-a-half wide! (Plus, he was told not to swing the bat.) Veeck had to show the umpire a copy of Gaedel's contract to prove he was eligible to play. Bill is famous for a lot of his creative promotions, including Disco Demolition Night, but this stunt was the first one to get him national attention. Bill was a great guy. Anyone who played for him thought he was kindhearted to a fault, and he had an enthusiasm for the game that was unparalleled.

Jerry Reuss, Ultimate Prankster

"Ladies and gentlemen, Mr. Nude!"

That's what I used to say almost every day in the White Sox clubhouse whenever Jerry Reuss was around. Jerry never had clothes on when he was in the clubhouse. I never saw anybody who walked around naked more than he did. I think it was just another one of the ways he went about keeping the team "loose."

We played together on a couple of bad White Sox teams in 1988 and 1989, at the tail end of his career and, come to think of it, kind of the beginning of the end for mine as well.

Jerry had a great career. He threw a no-hitter, pitched in the playoffs a few times, was second in the Cy Young voting one year, and made a couple All-Star teams—pretty good stuff. Heck, he played for 22 years and won 220 games as a big leaguer, so we're not just talking about your run-of-the-mill nudist here.

But with all the things he accomplished on the field, I think most of his teammates and coaches and definitely one manager will remember him for his off-the-field antics. No, Jerry didn't get in any real trouble—you were never going to read his name in the paper after a DUI or for tax evasion or anything like that. Jerry probably hasn't even had a parking ticket in his whole life. But he does have a devious mind. He's one of those lie-in-the-weeds kind of guys who goes almost unnoticed. Believe it or not, Reuss was the man behind all the crazy Dodgers teams of the 1980s, and when you put a guy like Jay Johnstone on the same team with him, nobody was safe from a prank.

Hot foots, shaving-cream pies, and putting Icy Hot in a guy's jock was kid stuff compared to the things Jerry would think up.

Part of his genius was that he rarely owned up to being behind the stunts—even today! Try to talk to him about it and all you'll get is a smile, then he'll put on his headphones and listen to one of the tens of thousands of classic rock songs he has on his iPod—nobody knows rock history like he does.

Anyway, everybody knew that Tommy Lasorda was one of Jerry's favorite targets. Jerry used to find new and creative ways to ruin any homemade dish that somebody might deliver to Tommy at the clubhouse just to make sure Tommy couldn't eat it. During one spring training, Lasorda found himself locked in his room and the mouthpiece missing from his hotel phone so he couldn't call anybody to come let him out. Seems somebody got up late at night and tied his hotel room's doorknob to a pole and Tommy couldn't budge it. Jerry swears to this day that it wasn't him and coyly hints it was Johnstone, but that's just because he knows Lasorda is still pissed about it!

Some say that ballplayers are all immature children who never want to grow up. Others say they just want to have a little fun and blow off some of the pressure that builds during a 162-game schedule. I agree—to all of it. I think for Jerry, who was such an inquisitive, intelligent guy, the four days off between his starts must have driven him crazy. He was trying to make sure his mind was put to good use during his downtime.

One day he noticed home-plate umpire Frank Pulli was in a foul mood, so he sent the batboy up to home plate between innings with a cup of coffee for Frank. He snickered as Pulli dumped the coffee out. So Jerry waited an inning or two and then got another idea. He took one of the game balls and wrote "Frank, God Bless You, Tommy Lasorda" on it. He gave the ball to the same batboy and told him to give it to Pulli when he brought balls out to him for his ball pouch.

Well, Pulli never noticed the ball had been written on and actually put it in play when he threw it to Tom Niedenfeur to pitch with after a foul ball. Two pitches later that ball got fouled off into the players' wives' section of the stands.

But the story gets better.

When Niedenfeur got the side out, he came and sat down right next to Reuss on the bench and said, "Jerry, you'll never believe what just happened. I just used a ball that had writing on it." Jerry just looked at him coolly and said, "I know, Tom, every ball has writing on it. The commissioner's name is on it, and the league's president's name...."

"No," Niedenfeur said, "I mean real writing, like somebody else wrote on the ball."

Knowing full well what was going on, Jerry said, "That's odd," and figured the whole thing was over.

Shortly after the game, somebody told Jerry that Lasorda wanted him in his office. When somebody says that to you, it's never good news; either you're getting traded or sent down or you've done something wrong and you're in trouble.

It turns out that the ball that Jerry signed with Tommy's signature, the same ball that had been placed in Frank Pulli's ball bag, the same ball that got put into play and pitched by Tom Niedenfeur, and the same ball that got fouled into the stands behind home plate, was unbelievably caught by a guy named Frank!

This Frank was sitting close to Tommy Lasorda's wife and he showed her the ball in amazement. She knew something wasn't quite right, so she gave Tommy a call right after the game and told him the story.

Tommy went straight to Jerry Reuss, knowing that if something smelled funny, Jerry was likely behind it. So Reuss got chewed out again.

The next night, Pulli and his umpiring crew gave Reuss a stern talking to in the umpires' room before the game. They reprimanded him for defacing game balls and compromising the integrity of the game and all that stuff. Pulli wasn't serious, but Jerry didn't know that. Gotcha back!

Years later, Reuss sent a ballgirl over to Pulli, who was umpiring at first base, with another ball. This one read, "Frank, May God Bless You, Jerry Reuss."

This time Pulli laughed—which was all Jerry was after in the first place.

About the Authors

Steve Lyons played Major League Baseball for nine years and is a three-time Emmy award–winning analyst. He is currently a broadcaster with the Los Angeles Dodgers after spending 11 years at Fox Sports, where he covered the World Series, hosted the interview show Rewind, and anchored FSN's *National Sports Report*. He has also hosted radio shows based in Boston, Chicago, and Los Angeles, and is the author of *PSYCHOanalysis*. A former member of the Red Sox, White Sox, Braves, and Expos, he is one of only three players in major-league history to play all nine positions in a single game. A single father of three daughters—Kristen, 29, Kori, 22, and Alexandra, nine—and the proud grandfather of Anthony, eight, he currently resides in Southern California.

Burton Rocks is the coauthor of the *New York Times* bestseller *Me and My Dad: A Baseball Memoir*, about Yankees great Paul O'Neill and his father. A third-generation author, Rocks has published six books and cowrote Billy Wagner's exclusive 2006 playoff column for the *New York Post*. A Phi Beta Kappa graduate of Stony Brook University and graduate of Hofstra University School of Law, he owns his own boutique sports agency, Burton Rocks LTD. He serves on the Board of Governors at the Friars Club and is a member of the New York Athletic Club.